# NO
# OTHER
# GODS

ISBN:  979-8-9867392-0-5

To my wife who, like her namesake,
left home for an uncertain future
in unknown places.

*"Whither thou goest, I will go;*
*and where thou lodgest, I will lodge:*
*thy people shall be my people,*
*and thy God my God."*

Ruth 1:16 (KJV)

I am the lord your God,

who brought you out of the land

of Egypt,

out of the house of slavery;

you shall have no other gods before me.

Exodus 20:2-3

# Table of Contents

# Acknowledgements

Books like this aren't solitary endeavors. They incorporate a lifetime of learning gleaned from many sources. As rightly said, "We stand upon the shoulders of giants." Our individual accomplishments rest upon the collective wisdom of past generations. We simply build on what we've been given.

No one influences us more than our parents. For better or worse, their beliefs and values reside within our subconscious minds all our lives. My father, a Protestant fundamentalist, and my stepfather, a former Roman Catholic priest, profoundly influenced the course of my life. Both were dedicated Christians with strongly differing beliefs about the Christian faith. Those differences prompted the question of what to believe, which in turn led to my life's work.

Teachers are almost as influential as our parents but their impact on our lives too often goes unnoticed. I'm grateful to all the public school teachers who gave me an excellent foundation, and the college, seminary and graduate school professors who inspired me with their love of learning.

I also want to thank everyone who encouraged me to write this book. My late brother-in-law thought a book like this ought to be read by anyone contemplating a career in the church. Professor John M. Holcomb of the University of Denver (ret.), and Lt. Colonel David J. Bristow, Canadian Armed Forces (ret.), read early drafts of the manuscript and provided helpful feedback. I owe a special debt of gratitude to an acquisitions editor at a major denominational press without whose encouragement I might not have finished this book.

Above all, I wish to thank my wife. Her comments, questions and careful editing were invaluable. Her confidence in me never wavered, and that in itself has been the best help of all.

# Preface

Christianity is based on a man who lived in Palestine two thousand years ago. The man was a zealous Jew who proclaimed the coming end of this age in a fiery apocalypse that would bring God's kingdom in heaven down to earth. His preaching antagonized the religious establishment, posed a threat to Roman authorities and ultimately led to his execution.

But that wasn't the end of the matter. His followers said he didn't die, that he rose from the grave and ascended to heaven where he was enthroned next to almighty God himself![1] They claimed his death atoned for the sins of the world, and that everyone who believed in him would have eternal life. They thought he would reappear during their lifetime, and be acknowledged by everyone on earth as Lord of all. Later followers looked back on him as a divine being who left heaven and came to earth "incarnate" in human flesh. They also said that, after rising from the dead, he spent time on earth with his disciples before ascending into heaven.

Even greater claims were made. His followers eventually asserted that, in heaven, he and God were made of the "same substance," and together with a mysterious Holy Spirit formed a "trinity" of Gods which nonetheless comprised only one God. Moreover, in looking back at his life, they said he had been divine as well as human all the while he walked on earth.

These ideas belong to antiquity. Taken together, they portray a mythical being perfectly at home in the ancient world but completely out of place in ours. Collectively, they constitute the core beliefs of Christianity. The mythical figure created by

---

[1] Masculine pronouns used of God in this book are a literary convenience to avoid awkward sentences. They're anthropomorphisms that refer to God as if "he" were a man.

these beliefs bears little resemblance to the actual historical figure of Jesus.[1]

**The divine Christ is an intellectual abstraction shaped by ecclesiastical dogmas.** Yet this is who, or rather what, Christians worship. To see the real Jesus, the historical Jesus of Nazareth, the dogmas defining him as God need to be stripped away.

The "faith of our fathers" is based on a false image of Jesus. Devout Christians will find that upsetting, but it should reassure all who question the dogmas of Christ's divinity. Truth has an astringent quality. It frees us from ignorance, superstition and falsehoods of every kind. That's why I wrote this book. It's for all who've left Eden and look back, knowing they can't return.

---

[1] The claim is sometimes made that Jesus never existed. That assertion, however, is implausible. Religions don't originate in a vacuum, and they aren't produced by committees. Great religious movements began with extraordinary individuals who saw life *sub specie aeternitatis*—from the standpoint of eternity. One might just as well contend that Abraham and Moses never existed, that Buddhists invented Siddhartha Gautama and Muslims concocted the prophet Mohammed, as to say that Jesus never existed. The proof of the historical existence of these figures is in the movements they left behind.

# Foreword

## The Past in Perspective

The past is never past. It reaches into the present, influencing everything we think and do. Genes inherited from our earliest ancestors determine our physical and mental characteristics. The aftermath of wars and accidents stays with us all our lives. Our successes and failures never leave us. We're filled with nostalgia by thoughts of bygone days. The effects others have had on us, and those we've had on others, live on. The love, or abuse, of a parent is never forgotten. Steel bars are constant reminders of a prisoner's past mistakes. Veterans re-live past battles in terrifying nightmares to the end of their days. And what about us? What would our lives be like now if we had chosen another career or a different spouse? So, the past never ends. The present is simply its leading edge, a compendium of everything we ever did or failed to do. Regret and self-pity are worthless. Accepting the past and, if possible, making amends for it is the best we can do.

Civilization itself is built upon the past. The accomplishments of each generation are laid like rows of bricks atop one another. Philosophers and mathematicians, engineers and scientists, politicians and poets, playwrights, artists, musicians and myriads of other long forgotten people forged the paths we tread. So again, the past is never past. It's a continuum that stretches back to the dawn of time.

Nevertheless, despite its impact upon the present, the past itself is irrecoverable. What were Pompeii and Herculaneum like before they were buried in ash by Mount Vesuvius in 79 CE? Mute vestiges of their existence are all that remain. The zeitgeist of an age is fleeting. We can't experience life the way it was lived by people in the past. The cobblestone streets of ancient cities are silent now, but what were they like in their

day? When merchants hawked their wares and ruffians, scalawags, beggars, soldiers, priests and prostitutes jostled along the way?  When dogs barked and donkeys brayed and children laughed and played in the afternoon sun?  When aromas of baking bread and roasting meat wafted through the air, along with the stench of raw sewage laying in the gutters?  What did people think about?  The latest news from Rome?  Their favorite gladiator?  A play in the amphitheater that evening or an upcoming chariot race?  What were their hopes?  Their fears?  What made them laugh?  What were their thoughts about politics and religion?  We can only speculate.  It's impossible to go back and walk in their sandals, think their thoughts or feel their feelings.  The spirit of an age is ephemeral.  As Heraclitus (535-475 BCE) observed, "No one steps into the same river twice."  Life, like a river, flows on.  We can't go back in time to places that no longer exist.

Nevertheless, despite being unable to experience life as actually lived in the past, we're still connected to our forbears.  Human emotions haven't changed.  Love and hate, anger and fear, jealousy, happiness and grief are still the same as ever.  The historical *contexts* of emotions change, but not the emotions themselves.  The behavior of animals shows that emotions exist across a broad biological spectrum.  From an evolutionary perspective, this indicates that feeling preceded thinking.  The simplest protozoa react to external forces acting upon them.  In like manner, early hominids reacted to danger long before they possessed the ability to conceptualize it.

Descartes maintained that thinking was the fundamental datum of human existence: *"Cogito ergo sum"*— "I *think* therefore I am."  Rousseau, on the other hand, offered a counterdictum: "I *feel* therefore I am."  On a cognitive level, Descartes was correct, but at a deeper, existential level Rousseau was right.  So, in terms of our emotions, we're no different from our ancestors.  We feel what they felt, and that continuity enables us to see ourselves in them.

*Ideas*, on the other hand, are timebound.  They arise at certain points in history and express the thoughts of a particular age.  Some ideas, of course, are never outdated.  Euclidian geometry, Pythagorean theorems and Aristotelian logic are still as valid as ever, and Roman law and Greek philosophy underpin our thinking to the present day.

Ancient *cosmological* ideas, however, are a different matter. They originated long ago in a prescientific age and have no relevance to the present. Gods were responsible for everything that happened in antiquity. Lightning bolts were seen as their arrows and thunder was heard as the sound of their voice. Gods were responsible for solar eclipses, earthquakes, droughts and floods, and determined the size and health of harvests, flocks and herds. Magicians cajoled their favor. Spirits inhabited rock formations, trees, rivers and springs. Irascible sprites called "jinn" harassed lost travelers. Demons invaded people's bodies, making them physically and mentally ill. Superstition guided a person's every decision, and fate determined their destiny.

The earth was flat, not round—and it didn't circle the sun. The sun circled earth. Outer space was an immense ocean kept from drowning the earth by a dome, a "firmament," fixed high in the sky. Twinkling stars were the dead. And on it goes. . . Mythical ideas provided explanations for otherwise inexplicable phenomena. The modern world could never have been envisioned by people living in that age.

That was the worldview within which the dogmas of Christ's divinity were formulated. The mythical and philosophical ideas they express were common in the ancient world. They didn't drop from heaven and aren't eternally valid. They originated in the minds of men who lived two thousand years ago. But time moves on. Life changes. We don't live in antiquity. The dogmas of a divine Christ belong to an age that disappeared with the wind.

# PART ONE
# EARLY DOGMAS

# Introduction
## From History to Dogmas

Trying to see the real Jesus, Jesus of Nazareth, is like staring into dense fog. The historical figure of Jesus is hard to discern because it's hidden behind ecclesiastical dogmas that proclaim his divinity. Jesus himself, however, never claimed to be divine. As a Jew, he worshipped one God alone and never intended to found a new religion, much less become the object of one. That would have been blasphemy to pious Jews like Jesus. The dogmas of his divinity were conceived long after his death and, like barnacles on the hull of a ship, have clung to him ever since. Taken together, they comprise a Christological myth barely tied to history.

The dogmas of Christ's divinity took shape in the early centuries of the Common Era. They were simple beliefs at first, but later evolved into philosophical statements. An approximate timeline can be drawn for when they appeared based on two criteria: *proximity* to Jesus' lifetime, and *complexity* of thought. Measured by those standards, the dogmas of Christ's resurrection and atonement came first, followed by the dogmas of his second coming, pre-existence, incarnation, virgin birth and ascension to heaven. The dogmas of the trinity and Christ's two natures came last, capping a steady march toward philosophy that ultimately removed Jesus from the realm of history altogether.

Unlearning is essential to learning. Falsehoods need to be exposed, erroneous ideas discredited and presuppositions questioned in order to advance knowledge in any field of study, including religion. Christianity, as a system of dogmatic beliefs, is like a crustacean unchanged for eons. If we wish to see Jesus, the dogmas of his divinity need to be stripped away.

# Chapter One
# RESURRECTION

Ancient people attributed the dying and sprouting of plants in the fall and spring to the death and rebirth of agricultural gods. Crops were harvested in Sumeria when Tammuz died every fall. They were harvested in Syria when Adonis died in the fall, and planted when he came back to life in the spring. In Egypt, Osiris came out of the ground in the spring and returned to it every fall. The Greek goddess Persephone spent six months of each year above ground, and six within it. The death and rebirth of crops in the fall and spring of the year mirrored the dying and rising of these and other gods.

This natural cycle undoubtedly prompted the idea of resurrection. If plants came back to life, why couldn't humans do the same? Greeks were repulsed by the thought of reanimated corpses, and spoke instead of immortal souls. The possibility of resuscitation was nevertheless acknowledged on the basis of meritorious deeds. Plato spoke of a woman who died for her husband, "and so noble did this action of hers appear to the gods that among the many who have done virtuously she is one of the very few to whom they have granted the privilege of returning alive to earth."[1] Asclepius, the Greek god of healing, was said to have raised people from the dead. So, long before Jesus died, the concept of resurrection was well known.

## The Gospels

The story of Jesus' resurrection started with Mark, the earliest written gospel.[2] Mark contains oral traditions that circulated by word of mouth before being written down. The authors of

---

[1] The Dialogues of Plato (trans. B. Jowett; New York: Random House, 1937, Seventeenth Printing), 308.
[2] Mark was written shortly after the destruction of Jerusalem in 70 CE. Matthew and Luke were written a decade or so later, and John appeared in the last decade of the first century.

2

Matthew and Luke copied Mark—cut, pasted and rearranged—in writing their own gospels.[1] Comparing those gospels to Mark shows how easily the story of Jesus' resurrection evolved.[2]

# Mark

Mark describes the Easter event as follows:

*When the sabbath was over, Mary Magdalene, and Mary the mother of James, and Salome bought spices, so that they might go and anoint him. And very early on the first day of the week, when the sun had risen, they went to the tomb. They had been saying to one another, who will roll away the stone for us from the entrance to the tomb?" When they looked up, they saw that the stone, which was very large, had already been rolled back. As they entered the tomb, they saw a young man, dressed in a white robe, sitting on the right side; and they were alarmed. But he said to them, "Do not be alarmed; you are looking for Jesus of Nazareth, who was crucified. He has been raised; he is not here. Look, there is the place they laid him. But go, tell his disciples and Peter that he is going ahead of you to Galilee; there you will see him, just as he told you."[3]*

# Matthew

Matthew repeats Mark:

*After the sabbath, as the first day of the week was dawning, Mary Magdalene and the other Mary went to see the tomb. And suddenly there was a great earthquake; for an angel of the Lord, descending from heaven, came and rolled back the stone and sat on it. His appearance was like lightning, and his clothing white as snow. For fear of him the guards shook and became like dead men. But the angel said to the women,*

---

[1] The authors also relied upon another written source, now lost, called "Q," as well as sources ("M" in Matthew and "L" in Luke) unique to each gospel.
[2] The non-canonical accounts in the New Testament Apocrypha demonstrate the growth of wildly imaginative stories about Jesus' birth and childhood.
[3] Mark 16:1-7.

*"Do not be afraid; I know that you are looking for Jesus who was crucified. He is not here; for he has been raised, as he said. Come, see the place where he lay. Then go quickly and tell his disciples, 'He has been raised from the dead, and indeed he is going ahead of you to Galilee; there you will see him.'"*[1]

Three women ("Mary Magdalene, Mary the mother of James, and Salome") go to the tomb in Mark, but only two go to it in Matthew ("Mary Magdalene and the other Mary").

Mark doesn't explain how the stone got moved away from the tomb's entrance, but Matthew says, "And suddenly there was a great earthquake; for an angel of the Lord, descending from heaven, came and rolled back the stone and sat on it."

Mark's "young man, dressed in a white robe" sitting inside the tomb becomes an angel whose appearance "was like lightning, and his clothing white as snow" in Matthew.

Mark says nothing about Roman soldiers guarding the tomb, but Matthew states they were there.

Mark ends abruptly, saying the women "went out and fled from the tomb, for terror and amazement had seized them; and they said nothing to anyone, for they were afraid."[2] That conclusion was unacceptable to the author of Matthew,[3] who replaced it with this:

*So they left the tomb quickly with fear and great joy, and ran to tell his disciples. Suddenly Jesus met them and said*

---

[1] Matt 28:1-10.

[2] Mark 16:8.

[3] Mark's abrupt conclusion suggests that its original ending was lost. Early Christians fixed the apparent problem by adding "more appropriate" endings, several of which survive. One is grandiloquent: *"And all that had been commanded them they told briefly to those around Peter. And afterward Jesus himself sent out through them, from east to west, the sacred and imperishable proclamation of eternal salvation."* A longer ending (16:9-20) combines elements from the conclusions of Matthew and Luke with features from the Acts of the Apostles.

*"Greetings!" And they came to him, took hold of his feet, and worshipped him. Then Jesus said to them, "Do not be afraid; go and tell my brothers to go to Galilee; there they will see me."* [1]

This is less disjointed and more positive than Mark's ending. Note that Jesus' risen body is portrayed here as a physical body, with feet to be held.

Matthew adds a curious detail about the disciples' meeting Jesus in Galilee: "When they saw him, they worshipped him; *but some doubted.*"[2] The afterthought, "but some doubted," is telling. Not all early Christians believed Christ rose from the dead.[3]

# Luke

Luke embellishes Mark:

*But on the first day of the week, at early dawn, they came to the tomb, taking the spices that they had prepared. They found the stone rolled away from the tomb, but when they went in, they did not find the body. While they were per-plexed about this, suddenly two men in dazzling clothes stood beside them. The women were terrified and bowed their faces to the ground, but the men said to them, "Why do you look for the living among the dead? He is not here, but has risen. Remember how he told you, while he was still in Galilee, that the Son of Man must be handed over to sinners, and be crucified, and on the third day rise again." Then they remembered his words, and returning from the tomb, they told all this to the eleven and to all the rest. Now it was Mary Magdalene, Joanna, Mary the mother of James, and the other women with them who told this to the apostles. But these words seemed to them an idle tale, and they did not*

---

[1] Matt 28:8-10.

[2] Matt 28:17 (my italics).

[3] Paul confronted this problem in Corinth: "Now if Christ is proclaimed as raised from the dead, how can some of you say there is no resurrection of the dead?" (1 Cor 15:12)

5

*believe them. But Peter got up and ran to the tomb; stooping and looking in, he saw the linen cloths by themselves; then he went home, amazed at what had happened.*[1]

Luke agrees with Mark that "Mary Magdalene and Mary the mother of James" went to the tomb, but they're accompanied by Joanna instead of Salome. "Other women" are also said to have gone with them.

Luke, like Mark, says nothing about how the stone at the tomb's entrance got moved. Inside the tomb, Mark's "young man, dressed in a white robe" becomes "two men in dazzling clothes."

Mark refers to Jesus as "Jesus of Nazareth," but Luke gives him the honorific title, "Son of Man."[2]

Jesus doesn't know in Mark of the fate awaiting him in Jerusalem, but he's well aware of it in Luke.[3]

Like the person who wrote Matthew, the author of Luke replaced Mark's truncated conclusion with one of his own. The women don't flee the tomb in fear; they report back "to the eleven and to all the rest," who dismiss their words as "an idle tale" (the women were presumably hysterical!) Nevertheless, Peter sets off to see for himself. Luke's deviations from Mark, like those in Matthew, point to the inventiveness of its author. Early Christians felt no obligation to be objective, and "improved" the story of Jesus' resurrection as they wished.

Luke has a strange story that isn't found in the other gospels.[4] As two of Jesus' disciples walked away from Jerusalem after his crucifixion, they were joined by a stranger asking for

---

[1] Luke 24: 1-12.
[2] Referring to Jesus as "Jesus of Nazareth" identified him as the Jesus who lived in Nazareth as opposed to men with the same name who lived elsewhere. "Son of Man" was a title conferred upon Jesus after his death.
[3] Luke has three references to Jesus' foreknowledge of his fate (Luke 9:22, 18:31-33 and 24:6) but, as argued in my next book, these were invented.
[4] Luke 24:13-43.

6

news from the city. Incongruously, after being told of Jesus' death, he "interpreted to them the things about himself in all the scriptures." As day wore on, the disciples invited the stranger to stay the night with them. But after they stopped, things got weird:

*When he was at the table with them, he took bread, blessed and broke it, and gave it to them. Then their eyes were opened, and they recognized him; and he vanished from their sight.*[1]

This story originated in oral tradition. It's an apocryphal tale about Jesus' walking incognito with two of his disciples after rising from the dead. Nothing seems amiss until evening. But then, in sharing bread, they suddenly recognize the stranger— who immediately disappears into thin air!

Astonished, they run back to the city to tell the other disciples about seeing Jesus alive. Then, as they spoke, Jesus appears out of nowhere. "They were startled and terrified, and thought that they were seeing a ghost," but Jesus reassures them:

*Why are you frightened, and why do doubts arise in your hearts? Look at my hands and my feet; see that it is I myself. Touch me and see; for a ghost does not have flesh and bones as you see that I have.*[2]

To show that he wasn't a ghost, he asks for something to eat. So, "They gave him a piece of broiled fish, and he took it and ate in their presence."

Like Mark and Matthew, Luke represents Jesus' risen body as his crucified body—appetite and all! So, Jesus wasn't an apparition. Despite appearing and disappearing at will, he was the very person who died on the cross.

---

[1] Luke 24:30-31.
[2] Luke 24:38-39.

# John

The Gospel of John captures oral traditions not found in the other gospels. One of those traditions emphasizes Mary Magdalene's supposed role in the day's events:

*Early on the first day of the week, while it was still dark, Mary Magdalene came to the tomb and saw that the stone had been removed from the tomb. So she ran and went to Simon Peter and the other disciple, the one whom Jesus loved, and said to them, "They have taken the Lord out of the tomb, and we do not know where they have laid him." Then Peter and the other disciple set out and went toward the tomb. The two were running together, but the other disciple outran Peter and reached the tomb first. He bent down to look in and saw the linen wrapping lying there, but he did not go in. Then Simon Peter came, following him, and went into the tomb. He saw the linen wrappings lying there, and the cloth that had been on Jesus' head, not lying with the linen wrappings but rolled up in a place by itself. Then the other disciple, who reached the tomb first, also went in, and he saw and believed; for as yet they did not understand the scripture, that he must rise from the dead. Then the disciples returned to their homes.* [1]

The fourth gospel says that Mary Magdalene was the first person to find the tomb empty. She accompanies other women to the tomb in the first three gospels, but here she's alone. The stone has been moved aside from the tomb's entrance, allowing her to peer inside and see that it's empty. Alarmed, she runs to tell Peter and "the disciple whom Jesus loved" that Jesus' body is gone, whereupon both race to the tomb to see for themselves. The "beloved disciple" arrives before Peter but waits for him to enter the tomb first before going in himself. Then, at a loss, both men leave.

---

[1] John 20:1-10.

Mary Magdalene, however, stays behind, distraught and grieving at the empty tomb. Then, as she finally rises to leave, she sees a man who appears to be a gardener. "Sir," she implores, "if you have carried him away, tell me where you have laid him, and I will take him away." The "gardener," however, calls to her by name, and she immediately recognizes the voice. "Rabbouni!" she cries, reaching out to embrace him. But Jesus backs away. "Do not hold on to me, because I have not yet ascended to the Father." Holding Jesus would have kept him from rising to heaven. Here, therefore, as elsewhere in the gospels, Jesus' risen body is portrayed as a physical body.

John ends with two accounts that only appear in that gospel. The first pictures Jesus' disciples cowering in a locked house "for fear of the Jews" after Jesus' execution. As they huddled together, Jesus "came and stood among them and said, 'Peace be with you,'" and showed them the wounds in his hands and side.[1] Thomas, however, wasn't there when that happened, and refused to believe that Jesus had really appeared. Days later, when all the disciples were together, Jesus reappeared and spoke directly to Thomas: "Put your finger here and see my hands. Reach out your hand and put it in my side. Do not doubt but believe." Astonished, Thomas exclaims, "My Lord and my God!" As in the first three gospels, Jesus' risen body is here described as a physical body—which, nonetheless, could pass through locked doors!

The second account occupies the entire last chapter in John.[2] Like the endings added to Mark, it was appended to John to "improve" its original conclusion.[3] The disciples are portrayed as having resumed their old occupation as fishermen while

---

[1] John 20:19-29.
[2] John 21:1-25.
[3] The fourth gospel originally ended at John 20:30-31:
   *Now Jesus did many other signs in the presence of his disciples, which are not written in this book. But these are written so that you may come to believe that Jesus is the Messiah, the Son of God, and that through believing you may have life in his name.*

9

waiting for Jesus to arrive in Galilee.[1] They were returning to shore after fishing all night without catching a single fish when a man on the beach called to them to cast their net on the other side of the boat. They followed that suggestion, and were amazed to find their net full of fish! Seeing this, they realize that the man standing on the beach was none other than Jesus himself. After pulling ashore, they see a charcoal fire, and broiled fish and baked bread waiting to be eaten. Once finished, they listen to Jesus as he instructs Peter to "tend my sheep," and tells him how he will die.

This is the grand finale of all Jesus' post-resurrection appearances. It's an apocryphal tale about a miraculous catch of fish that shows Jesus lighting a fire, broiling fish, baking bread and speaking at length with Peter. It's highly imaginative and emphasizes the physicality of Jesus' risen body more than any other post-resurrection story in the gospels.

# The Apostle Paul

Unlike the gospels, Paul didn't think of the risen Jesus as having a physical body. That's a critical realization inasmuch as his letters appeared earlier than the earliest written gospel.[2] Paul's letters express beliefs held by the first Christians, whereas the gospels represent later stages in the development of those beliefs. The nature of Jesus' resurrected body is a case in point.

The earliest reference to Jesus' resurrection appears in First Corinthians, which Paul wrote in the spring of 54 or 55 CE:[3]

---

[1] The starting point for this tale is found in Mark (14:28; 16:7) and Matthew (28:7,10,16), both of which say the risen Jesus would meet his disciples in Galilee.
[2] Paul wrote in the mid-fifties of the first century. Mark, the earliest gospel, was written shortly after 70 CE. Matthew and Luke were composed over a decade after Mark, and John wasn't written until the final decade of the first century.
[3] Werner Georg Kümmel, *Introduction to the New Testament* (trans. Howard Clark Kee; Nashville: Abingdon Press, 1975), 279.

10

*For I handed on to you as of first importance what I in turn had received: that Christ died for our sins in accordance with the scriptures, and that he was buried, and that he was raised on the third day in accordance with the scriptures, and that he appeared to Cephas, then to the twelve. Then he appeared to more than five hundred brothers and sisters at one time, most of whom are still alive, though some have died. Then he appeared to James, then to all the apostles. Last of all, as to one untimely born, he appeared also to me.*[1]

## The Third Day

"Raised on the third day in accordance with the scriptures" referred to biblical passages interpreted as prophecies of Christ's resurrection.

Paul might have been thinking of **Psalm 16:10**:

*For you do not give me up to Sheol,*
*or let your faithful one see the Pit.*

He might also have had **Hosea 6:2** in mind:

*After two days he will revive us;*
*on the third day he will raise us up.*

This is poetic parallelism in which the second line rephrases the first for emphasis. In this case, "two days" is rephrased as "the third day." Neither was meant literally. Both were used poetically to indicate a short period of time. Repetition like this occurs throughout Hebrew poetry.[2]

Paul might also have been thinking of **Jonah 1:17**:

*But the Lord provided a large fish to swallow up Jonah; and Jonah was in the belly of the fish three days and three nights.*

This wasn't a fish tale in those days! It was taken literally. Being "in the belly of the fish three days and three nights"

---

[1] 1 Cor 15:3-8.
[2] Prov 30:15,18,21,29 and Amos 1:3,9,11,13; 2:1,4,6 are just a few of hundreds of other examples in Hebrew scripture.

11

corresponded with Hosea's "third day," and prefigured Christ's own escape from death.

These and other passages may have been the source of saying Christ was raised "in accordance with the scriptures."

Three day time frames are frequent in Hebrew scripture. Three day journeys are taken,[1] but never any one, two, four or five day journeys. Three day time frames are found in various contexts.[2] The repetitiveness of this pattern indicates that it stood for a brief but otherwise unspecified period of time.

"Forty" was used in a similar sense. Rain fell on Noah's ark "forty days and forty nights."[3] The Israelites wandered in the wilderness for "forty years."[4] Moses spent "forty days and forty nights" on Mount Sinai.[5] Five Israelite kings had reigns of "forty years."[6] "Forty years" of rest followed major military campaigns in Canaan.[7] Jesus was tempted by the devil in the wilderness for "forty days."[8] "Forty" in a figurative sense was used in other contexts as well.[9]

The repetitiveness of this pattern shows that "forty" wasn't a precise chronological measurement. It was a generalization, a shorthand way of saying "a long time" when the actual time of

---

[1] Gen 30:36, 42:17; Exod 3:18, 5:3, 8:27, 15:22; Num 10:33, 33:8; Jonah 3:3.
[2] Gen 40:13,19; Exod 10:22,23; Josh 1:11, 2:16,22, 3:2, 9:16; Judg 14:14, 19:4; 1 Sam 9:20, 30:12,13; 2 Sam 20:4, 24:13; 1 Kgs 12:5; 2 Kgs 2:17; 1 Chr 12:39, 21:12; 2 Chr 10:5, 20:25; Ezra 8:15,32, 10:8,9; Neh 2:11; Esth 4:16.
[3] Gen 7:4,12; 8:6.
[4] Exod 16:35; Num 13:25, 14:33,34, 32:13; Deut 2:7, 8:2,4, 29:5; Neh 9:21; Ps 95:10; Amos 2:10, 5:25; Acts 1:3, 7:42, 13:18; Heb 3:9,17.
[5] Ex 24:18, 34:28; Deut 9:9,11,18,25, 10:10; Acts 7:23,30,36.
[6] Acts 13:21 (Saul); 2 Sam 5:4, 1 Kgs 2:11, 1 Chr 29:27 (David); 1 Kgs 11:42, 2 Chr 9:30 (Solomon); 2 Kgs 12:1 (Jehoash); 2 Chr 24:1 (Joash).
[7] Judg 3:11, 5:31, 8:28, 13:1.
[8] Matt 4:2; Mark 1:13; Luke 4:2. This story evoked the Israelites' ordeal in the wilderness, and Moses' lack of food and water on Mount Sinai.
[9] See, for example, Gen 50:3; 1 Sam 4:18, 17:16; 1 Kgs 19:8; Ezek 4:6, 29:11,12,13; Jonah 3:4; Acts 4:22.

doing something wasn't known. Similar generalizations appear elsewhere in Hebrew scripture, as in the exaggerated numbers of men said to have fought in battles.

It's clear from this, therefore, that "three days" was a figure of speech taken literally by the earliest Christians.

# Visions

Paul wrote that Christ:

> ... *appeared to Cephas, then to the twelve. Then he appeared to more than five hundred brothers and sisters at one time ... Then he appeared to James, then to all the apostles. Last of all, as to one untimely born, he appeared also to me.*[1]

What did Paul mean by saying Jesus "appeared"? Did these people see Jesus in the flesh, or a *vision* of him?

**Paul believed that Jesus' body became "a life-giving spirit" when he rose from the dead.**[2] This belief indicates that Paul and the others saw *visions* of Jesus rather than his actual body. Paul may have had his experience on the Damascus road in mind when he said, "Last of all, as to one untimely born, he appeared also to me." Paul was Saul, a zealous Pharisee, before becoming a Christian. He was on his way to Damascus to arrest deviant Jews who believed in Christ when his life changed forever. Acts recounts what happened:

> *Now as he was going along and approaching Damascus, suddenly a light from heaven flashed around him. He fell to the ground and heard a voice saying to him, "Saul, Saul,*

---

[1] 1 Cor 15:5-8.

[2] *"If there is a physical body, there is also a spiritual body. Thus it is written, 'The first man, Adam, became a living being'; the last Adam became a life-giving spirit."* (1 Cor 15:44b-45) The "last Adam" in this passage clearly refers to Jesus.

The "Spirit of Christ" and the "Spirit of the Lord" are indistinguishable from the "Holy Spirit" and the "Spirit of God" in scripture (e.g. Acts 16:7; Rom 8:9; 2 Cor 3:17-18; Gal 4:6; Phil 1:19; 1 Pet 1:11; Rev 19:10).

*why do you persecute me?" He asked, "Who are you, Lord?" The reply came, "I am Jesus, whom you are persecuting. But get up and enter the city, and you will be told what you are to do."*[1]

Blinded, Paul was led by hand into Damascus, where he regained his sight three days later.[2]

Were the visions seen by Paul and others nothing more than subjective psychological experiences? Visions can be as real as reality itself. Loved ones, for instance, are sometimes seen after they've died. Can visions like those be dismissed as mere psychic phenomena, or do they point to something beyond themselves?

Visions have changed world history. Paul's vision on the Damascus road set the future course of western civilization. He established churches throughout Asia Minor and defined nascent Christianity in letters written back to those churches. And it all started with a vision on a dusty road!

The Roman Emperor Constantine reputedly saw a vision of the cross in the sky with the words, *"In Hoc Signo Vinces"*— "In this sign conquer"—before winning a momentous battle against Maxentius in October, 312 CE. His victory at the Milvian Bridge outside Rome marked a turning point in world history. Christianity was legalized and named the official religion of the Roman Empire before the end of the fourth century.[3] The rest, as they say, is history. Christianity spread north from Italy

---

[1] Acts 9:3-6.

[2] It's worth noting that Paul suffered from an eye disease:
*You know that it was because of a physical infirmity that I first announced the gospel to you; though my condition put you to the test, you did not scorn or despise me, but welcomed me as an angel of God . . . . For I testify that, had it been possible, you would have torn out your eyes and given them to me.* (Gal 4:13-15)

[3] The Edict of Thessalonica, issued by Theodosius I in 380 CE, made Christianity the official religion of the Roman Empire. Paganism itself was outlawed in 392 CE.

into Europe and then to the ends of the earth. Church history is filled with examples of such life-changing visons.

But visions aren't restricted to religion. They've inspired literary works and scientific advances as well. Mary Shelley wrote *Frankenstein* after a terrifying nightmare. Robert Louis Stevenson had a nightmare that resolved the plot of *The Strange Case of Dr. Jekll and Mr. Hyde.* Paul McCartney composed *Yesterday*, one of the Beetles' best known songs, in a dream.

Still another nightmare solved a problem with inventing sewing machines. Savages were pursuing Elias Howe with spears that had holes in their tips, which suggested putting holes in the tips of the needles of his new machine to guide the thread. Niels Bohr saw planets circling the sun in a dream, and then

pictured electrons circling the nucleus of an atom. Albert Einstein had a dream in which stars changed their positions in the sky as he sledded down a snowy mountain at night. Seeing the stars as not fixed in one position eventually led to his Theory of Relativity.[1]

Visions like these are baffling. What inspires them? Where do they come from? Are they "mere" psychological experiences, or something more?

The Swiss psychiatrist Carl Jung spoke of a "universal consciousness" binding all sentient creatures together, from insects and animals to humans, in an integrated web of mutual awareness. If that's correct, if a universal consciousness does exist, then visions like these might originate in a higher consciousness beyond our own. Dismissing them as nothing more than subjective psychological experiences is too simplistic. Like instinct, intuition and premonitions, visions point to something beyond themselves.

---

[1] Visions have inspired many scientific breakthroughs, including the chemical transmission of nerve impulses (Otto Loewi), the configuration of the Benzene molecule (August Kekulé) and the use of insulin to treat diabetes (Frederick Banting).

# Spiritual Bodies

When asked, "How are the dead raised? With what kind of body do they come?" Paul was unequivocal:

*Fool! What you sow does not come to life unless it dies. And as for what you sow, you do not sow the body that is to be, but a bare seed . . . So it is with the resurrection of the dead. What is sown is perishable, what is raised is imperishable. It is sown in dishonor, it is raised in glory. It is sown in weakness, it is raised in power.* **It is sown a physical body, it is raised a spiritual body** . . . .[1]

Germination mystified ancient people, making it the perfect illustration of physical bodies becoming spiritual bodies. Like seeds becoming plants, that transformation was a mystery.

Spiritual bodies were physical bodies in non-material form.[2] That sounds like an oxymoron until we think of ghosts, which every age and culture, including our own, commonly reports. People in ancient times simply assumed their existence.[3]

Paul wasn't talking about ghosts when he spoke of spiritual bodies, but apparitions of the dead point to what he may have had in mind. Spiritual bodies were unique to every individual because they retained that person's physical appearance and the accumulated memories of his or her life.

First century Jews believed in a *nephesh* (נפש) that retained a person's identity and memories. The *nephesh* was one's inner self outwardly expressed through his or her physical features and personality. As such, it differed from the Greek concept of immortal souls. The *nephesh* was holistic, a psychophysical unity of the whole person, whereas Greeks separated souls and bodies. The body acted as a "prison house" of the soul, entrapping it until a person died, whereupon the soul was freed from

---

[1] 1 Cor 15:36-37, 42-44 (my bolding).
[2] "Spiritual body" translates *sōma pneumatikon* in Greek.
[3] See Isa 29:4, Matt 14:26 and Mark 6:49.

its bondage to mortal flesh. Immortal souls without bodies were the opposite of a *nephesh* that united both.

Paul made sure his readers understood the illustration of seeds becoming plants:

*What I am saying, brothers and sisters, is this:* **flesh and blood cannot inherit the kingdom of God, nor does the perishable inherit the imperishable.**[1]

**This is the heart of the matter.** Think about these words in relation to Luke's story of Jesus' appearing to his disciples and saying:

*Look at my hands and my feet; see that it is I myself. Touch me and see; for a ghost does not have flesh and bones as you see that I have.*

Consider them in relation to the words spoken to Thomas in the Gospel of John:

*Put your finger here and see my hands. Reach out your hand and put it in my side.*

Compare them to the last chapter of John, to Jesus' lighting a fire, broiling fish, baking bread and conversing with Peter.

**Paul said nothing about the resurrected Jesus having a physical body.** As seen above, he spoke of the risen Jesus as being "a life-giving spirit."

So, how is this contradiction explained? Why do the gospels say the resurrected Jesus had a physical body when Paul clearly believed he was "a life-giving spirit"?

The answer is that early Christianity was a work in progress. The first Christians held various beliefs which time winnowed. The question of how, or in what form, Jesus rose from the dead is a case in point. The belief that Jesus became "a life-giving spirit" gave way over time to believing his body rose from the grave. The influx of Gentiles into the originally Jewish church

---

[1] 1 Cor 15:50 (my bolding).

17

probably accounts for this change. At any rate, it's clear that apostolic belief in Jesus as a "life-giving spirit" predates the later gospel stories of his body rising from a tomb, thus making it a more reliable indicator of what the first Christians actually believed.

## The Legend of an Empty Tomb

Paul never talked about an empty tomb. That's remarkable considering the fact that his preaching centered on Christ crucified and risen from the dead.[1] An empty tomb was a perfect fit for that message. But he never mentioned one. Not even once. And we have to ask why.

The obvious answer is that he hadn't *heard* of one. But how would that have been possible? How could he *not* have heard about something as crucial to his message as an empty tomb?

Paul's silence is all the more puzzling in light of the fact that he and Jesus' closest disciples were well acquainted. Three years after becoming a Christian, Paul traveled to Jerusalem, where he met with Peter and James "the Lord's brother" for fif-teen days.[2] He went back to Jerusalem fourteen years later to have "the acknowledged leaders" of the church check the accuracy of his preaching.[3] After listening to his missionary message, James, Peter and John certified it as correct. Later, in looking back at that meeting, Paul said they "contributed nothing" to his knowledge of Christ.[4]

Which poses an intriguing question. If Jesus' closest disciples certified Paul's preaching as correct, **why don't we read about an empty tomb in any of his letters?**

If Paul didn't know about an empty tomb when he met with James, Peter and John, they would have told him about it. After

---

[1] 1 Cor 1:18-24, 2:1-2.
[2] Gal 1:18-19.
[3] Gal 2:1-2.
[4] Gal 2:6. The RSV translates this (οὐδὲν προσανέθεντο) as "added nothing."

18

all, finding an empty tomb would have been the greatest moment of their lives, a supreme instant in which they realized that Jesus had risen from the dead. How could they *not* have shared an experience like that with Paul? It's inconceivable! They would have relished telling him about it.

The fact that Paul never mentioned an empty tomb points to his never having been *told* of one. If James, Peter and John had told him about an empty tomb, he would have included it in preaching about Christ rising from the dead. But we never hear about it, not even once, in any of his letters.

Paul's silence is evidence that Jesus' closest disciples never discussed an empty tomb when he met with them in Jerusalem. This can only mean that *they themselves didn't know of one.* And if *they*, his closest disciples, didn't know about an empty tomb, **it never existed**—despite its prominence in gospels written decades later.

But this raises another question. **If an empty tomb never existed, why was the story of one invented?**

*An empty tomb was proof of Christ's rising from the dead.*

If a body rose from a tomb, the tomb would be left empty. The logic was impeccable, and substantiated Jesus' rising from the dead. An empty tomb was evidence of his absence, and proof of his having risen from the grave.

The story was plausible, but fabricated. And we have to ask why.

# Spiritual Gifts

Every generation has beliefs that later generations disavow. Nevertheless, however unacceptable, such beliefs need to be addressed in order to form an accurate picture of an age. Ignoring them distorts history. Objectivity requires letting the past speak for itself. The phenomena of "spiritual gifts" in the Apostolic Age is a case in point. Whether such "gifts" were real can't be proven. Historical *references* to those gifts, however, are valid, and, if examined, allow the past to speak for itself.

19

**An empty tomb compensated for the loss of "spiritual gifts" at the end of the Apostolic Age.**

Charismatic experiences were normal in the primitive Church.[1] They were "gifts" of the Spirit bestowed by the risen Christ, and proof of his being alive.

Paul discussed these gifts in First Corinthians,[2] and enumerated them as follows:

*To each is given the manifestation of the Spirit for the common good. To one is given through the Spirit the utterance of **wisdom**, and to another the utterance of **knowledge** according to the same Spirit, to another **faith** by the same Spirit, to another gifts of **healing** by the one Spirit, to another the **discernment** of spirits, to another various kinds of **tongues**, to another the **interpretation** of tongues. All these are activated by one and the same Spirit, who allots to each one individually just as the Spirit chooses.[3]*

Whatever these "gifts" may have been, all were seen as manifestations of the Spirit of the risen Christ.

However, as the first Christians died, spiritual gifts died along with them. Paul's admonitions, "Do not forbid speaking in tongues"[4] and "Do not quench the Spirit,"[5] show that their use was being discouraged even before the end of the Apostolic Age.[6]

---

[1] Paul's letters contain over one hundred references to the Holy Spirit (**28** in Rom; **36** in 1 and 2 Cor; **16** in Gal; **11** in Eph and **12** in his other letters). Acts, while written long after Paul's time, nonetheless retains **57** direct references to the Spirit.

[2] Chapters 12, 13 and 14.

[3] 1 Cor 12:7-11 (my bolding).

[4] 1 Cor 15:45.

[5] 1 Thess 5:19.

[6] Some early Christians didn't know the Holy Spirit existed (Acts 19:1-7).

Spiritual gifts were forgotten as they died away. This is evident from the phenomenon of glossolalia,[1] or "speaking in tongues." Most early Christians spoke in tongues. Paul himself spoke in tongues,[2] and he encouraged everyone else to do the same: "Now I would like all of you to speak in tongues."[3] It's evident from statements like this that glossolalia was common in apostolic times.

Paul described the phenomenon in First Corinthians:

*If, therefore, the whole church comes together and all speak in tongues, and outsiders or unbelievers enter, will they not say that you are out of your mind?*[4]

"Speaking in tongues" was unintelligible. A room full of Christians speaking in tongues would have been bedlam, a cacophony of noise. Outsiders hearing this commotion would have thought them all crazy![5]

*What should be done then, my friends? When you come together, each one has a hymn, a lesson, a revelation, a tongue or an interpretation. Let all things be done for building up. If anyone speaks in a tongue, let there be only two or at most three, and each in turn; and let one interpret. But if there is no one to interpret, let them be silent in church and speak to themselves and God.*[6]

---

[1] The term in Greek is γλωσσολαλία (*glossolalia),* which combines γλωσσα (tongue, language) and λαλέω (to speak, talk, chat, prattle, make a sound).
[2] "I thank God that I speak in tongues more than all of you." (1 Cor 14:18)
[3] 1 Cor 14:3.
[4] 1 Cor 14:23.
[5] Pentecostalism is often seen as symptomatic of mental illness based on the behavior of unstable people under intense emotional stress. Such behavior, however, is atypical, and a caricature of the experience. Paul insisted that "The spirits of prophets are subject to the prophets." (I Cor 14:32) This means that prophets were in control of themselves. They weren't overpowered by the Spirit and didn't lose their senses. The Spirit supplemented, but didn't supplant, their mental faculties. The same was true of other spiritual gifts. Labeling the gifts themselves as pathological misconstrues the evidence and imposes our own value judgements on the phenomena.
[6] 1 Cor 14:26-28.

Comparing this description of tongues to the account of Pentecost in Acts shows how quickly the actual phenomenon was forgotten:

> When the day of Pentecost had come, (the disciples) were all together in one place. And suddenly from heaven there came a sound like the rush of a violent wind, and it filled the entire house where they were sitting. Divided tongues, as of fire, appeared among them, and a tongue rested on each of them. All of them were filled with the Holy Spirit and began to speak in other languages . . . . Amazed and astonished, (onlookers) asked, "Are not all these who are speaking Galileans? And how is it that we hear, each of us, in our own native language? Parthians, Medes, Elamites, and residents of Mesopotamia, Judea and Cappadocia, Pontus and Asia, Phrygia and Pamphylia, Egypt and the parts of Libya belonging to Cyrene, and visitors from Rome, both Jews and proselytes, Cretans and Arabs—in our own languages we hear them speaking about God's deeds of power."[1]

This is a stylized account that misundersands the phenomenon.[2] First Corinthians, written three decades earlier,[3] shows that glossolalia was *not* coherent speech in known languages. If not interpreted, it was incomprehensible.

The story of an empty tomb compensated for the loss of charismatic experiences that proved Christ was alive. It provided assurance, then and now, that Christ rose from the grave. But first generation Christians didn't need an empty tomb. Their faith didn't rest on second-hand reports or legends. It was grounded in the direct experience of Christ's Spirit.

---

[1] Acts 2:1-4, 7-11.
[2] The Gospel of John presents a different picture of how the disciples received the Spirit:
> Jesus said to them again, "Peace be with you. As the Father has sent me, so I send you." When he had said this, he breathed on them and said to them, "Receive the Holy Spirit." (John 20:21-22)
[3] Kümmel, *Introduction*, 186, 279.

Charismatic phenomena faded away as Christianity spread. Churches were few and far between in the beginning, with no set rules or formal beliefs. Exercising the gifts of the Spirit in an unstructured environment like that was perfectly acceptable. However, as the church continued to grow, order and control took precedence over the spontaneity of spiritual gifts.[1] Charismatic experiences were out of step with an increasingly institutionalized church and slowly faded away.

## Jesus' Body

The bodies of executed criminals were usually thrown into unmarked graves or lime pits. The corpses of insurrectionists were left rotting on their crosses as a warning against rebellion. Little was left after vultures and scavenger dogs got finished with them.[2] So, if someone should ask, "What happened to Jesus' body?" the answer, quite frankly, is that no one knows.

---

[1] The *Didache*, also known as *The Lord's Teaching Through the Twelve Apostles to the Nations*, addressed church order. Written in the late first century, it was the first book of its kind.

[2] Golgotha was called the "Place of the Skull" for good reason. As Jezebel's fate illustrates (2 Kgs 9:30-37), scavenger dogs left little else.

# Chapter Two
# ATONEMENT

**The dogma of Christ's atonement for sin reflects the ancient practise of animal sacrifice.** Animals were sacrificed in antiquity to placate gods who controlled everything that happened in the world. Sacrifices to these gods protected people from known and unknown perils, and served as the ancient equivalent of life and casualty insurance.

Homer's *Odyssey*, written in the eighth century BCE, describes one of those sacrifices.[1] The account begins with a prayer to the goddess Minerva:

> Holy queen, vouchsafe to send down thy grace upon myself, my good wife, and my children. In return, I will offer you in sacrifice a broad-browed heifer of a year old, unbroken, and never yet brought by man under the yoke.

After this prayer, the beast was sacrificed:

> When they had done praying and sprinkling the barley meal Thrasymedes dealt his blow, and brought the heifer down with a stroke that cut through the tendons at the base of the neck, whereupon the daughters and daughters-in-law of Nestor, and his venerable wife Eurydice screamed with delight. Then they lifted the heifer's head from off the ground, and Pisistratus cut her throat. When she had done bleeding and was quite dead, they cut her up.

---

[1] Robert Maynard Hutchins, Editor in Chief, vol 4: *Great Books of the Western World* (trans. Samuel Butler; Chicago: William Benton, 1952), vol. 4, 197.

# Sacrifices were Driven by Fear

Fear is palpable in an ancient Sumerian prayer known as the "Penitential Prayer to Every God":[1]

May the wrath of the heart of my god be pacified!
May the god who is unknown to me be pacified!
May the goddess who is unknown to me be pacified!
May the known and unknown god be pacified!
May the known and unknown goddess be pacified!

The prayer continues on like this for another forty-one lines!

Israelite religion was dominated by the same sense of angst. Ancient Israelites were told again and again, "You shall fear your God."[2] "The fear of God" wasn't a mere figure of speech in those days. Getting too close to God could prove fatal, as shown by Moses' warning to stay away from Mount Sinai while he was waiting for the Ten Commandments:

*Go down and warn the people not to break through to the Lord to look; otherwise many of them will perish. Even the priests who approach the Lord must consecrate themselves or the Lord will break out against them.*[3]

Getting too close to God was like being exposed to nuclear radiation. Sacred objects like the Ark of the Covenant were irradiated with holiness and could kill if touched.[4] The "fear of God"[5] wasn't simply an idea; it was felt viscerally. It eventually became a metaphor for wisdom,[6] but it was far more than that at first.

---

[1] Eugen Weber, ed., *The Western Tradition*, vol I: *From the Ancient World to Louis XIV* (Lexington, MA; D.C. Heath,1995, fifth edition), 38.

[2] The admonitions to fear God are concentrated in the ancient Holiness Code embedded in Leviticus (chapters 17-26).

[3] Exodus 19:21-22.

[4] 2 Sam 6:6-9. The story relates to the primitive power of taboo objects.

[5] Around 165 references to the "fear of God" appear in the Old Testament.

[6] Job 28:28; Ps 111:10; Prov 1:7, 9:10 and Micah 6:9, for example.

# Sacrifices were Food offered to the Gods

Sharing food is a universal gesture of good will, and offering it to gods was a way of obtaining their favor. In Mesopotamia:

> The altar was the table of the god, and every kind of food which men eat was laid upon it: meat (especialy mutton, but also beef and gazelle), poultry, fish, vegetables, fruit, sweets, and, of course, drink and bread.[1]

A Babylonian creation myth from the second millennium BCE describes the effect those offerings had upon the gods:

> . . . the gods scented the fragrance, the gods scented the lovely fragrance, the gods collected like flies around the sacrificer.[2]

This description is echoed in the Book of Genesis. Noah offered sacrifices after the flood, and when "the Lord smelled the pleasing odor" he vowed never again to flood the earth.[3] The story is crudely anthropomorphic, but was taken literally in ancient times.

Israelite sacrifices were based on the concept of offering food to the gods. According to the Book of Numbers:

> *The Lord spoke to Moses, saying: "Command the Israelites, and say to them: My offering, the food for my offerings by fire, my pleasing odor, you shall take care to offer to me at its appointed time."*[4]

Sacrifices followed a prescribed schedule.[5] Two labs were sacrificed each day, one at daybreak and the other at sunset. Four additional lambs were slain on the sabbath. Two bulls, a ram, seven lambs and a goat were sacrificed on the first day of

---

[1] Roland de Vaux, *Ancient Israel: Its Life and Institutions* (trans. John McHugh; New York: McGraw-Hill, 1961), 433.

[2] De Vaux, *Ancient Israel*, 433, citing the Gilgamesh Epic.

[3] Gen 8:21.

[4] Num 28:1-2.

[5] Num 28-29.

the month. A great many more were slain during religious festivals. Offerings of grain and wine accompanied each of these sacrifices.

Little of the animal was actually burned. Part of it rose to God in smoke, a portion went to the officiating priest, and the person who owned it got the rest. In effect, sacrifices operated like meat markets. Females and blemished males were offered up for individuals.[1] Fat from the intestines, kidneys, liver and tail was burned because, like blood, it contained life that had to go back to God.[2] Sacrifices established communion between God, the officiating priest and the person offering the animal.

A gift (*minḥah*) of unleavened bread, wine, grain, vegetables or fruit accompanied each sacrifice.[3] Incense pleased God and offset stench lingering around the altar. The "showbread" placed on tables outside the "Holy of Holies," the most sacred part of the temple, belongs here because it, too, was an edible gift for God.[4]

In Holocaust offerings, unlike others, the entire animal was burned (except for its skin). "Holocaust" transliterates the Greek noun (*holokautōma*), meaning "completely burned," which in turn translates a Hebrew verb (*'olah*) that means "to go up." The image this creates is of smoke rising and dissipating into thin air, conveying the burnt offering to an invisible God. The only anmals selected for holocaust offerings were unblemished males in perfect health.[5] Priests slit their throats and threw the gushing blood against the altar before burning the carcasses.

---

[1] These were called *zebah shᵉlamim.*
[2] De Vaux, *Ancient Israel*, 418. See also Lev. 3:16-17; 7:22-27. Fat may have been linked to blood because both are found in bone marrow.
[3] Lev 2.
[4] Lev 24:5-9.
[5] Lev 22:17-25.

# Sacrifices were Driven by Guilt as well as Fear

Guilt is often blamed on puritanical moral codes, but the "Penitential Prayer to Every God" shows that it's part of the human condition.[1]  The angst in that prayer is palpable:

> An offense against my god I have unwittingly committed.
> A transgression against my goddess I have unwittingly done.
> O Lord, my sins are many, great are my iniquities! . . .
> The sin which I have sinned, turn to mercy!
> The iniquity which I have committed,
>     let the wind carry away!
> My many transgressions tear off like a garment!
> My god, my sins are seven times seven; forgive my sins!
> My goddess, my sins are seven times seven; forgive my sins!
> Known and unknown god, my sins are seven times seven;
>     forgive my sins!
> Known or unknown goddess, my sins are seven times seven;
>     forgive my sins![2]

Two types of sacrifices (*ḥaṭṭa'th* and *'asham*) atoned for sin in ancient Israel.  Blood played an even greater part in these sacrifices than in others:

> When the sacrifice was offered for the high priest or for the entire people, there were three successive rites: the priest who is performing the sacrifice first collected the blood, entered into the Holy Place and there sprinkled the blood seven times against the veil which curtains off the Holy of Holies; next, he rubbed blood upon the corners of the altar of incense, which stood before the veil; thirdly, he poured out the rest of the blood at the foot of the altar of holocausts.[3]

---

[1] Empathy and remorse are normal human feelings.  The inability to feel them characterizes sociopathic behavior, which is classified by the Diagnostic and Statistical Manual of Mental Disorders, Fifth Edition as Antisocial Personality Disorder (DSM-5 301.7).

[2] Weber, *The Western Tradition*, 39-40.

[3] De Vaux, *Ancient Israel*, 419.

Ancient Israelites thought that life resided in blood. That idea arose quite naturally from seeing people and animals "bleed to death" as they lost blood.

Life belonged to God. An animal's "life-blood," therefore, was sacred, and couldn't be eaten. Leviticus states the rule:

> *If anyone of the house of Israel or of the aliens who reside among them eats any blood, I will set my face against that person who eats blood, and will cut that person off from the people.* ***For the life of the flesh is in the blood****; and I have given it to you for making atonement for your lives on the altar; for, as life, it is the blood that makes atonement.*[1]

Splashing the blood of a sacrificed beast against the altar conveyed its life back to God.

An animal's owner got none of its meat in sacrifices for sin. God's representatives, the priests, got it all. That was the price paid for sin. When these sacrifices were made for a high priest or the community at large, the animal was completely burned and no one got any part of it. Sacrifices for sin were especially popular on Yom Kippur, Israel's great Day of Atonement.

A curious rite performed on Yom Kippur involved "a goat for Azazael." Lots were drawn between two male goats, one of which was sacrificed and the other sent off to Azazael, the desert demon. Leviticus describes the ritual:

> *Then Aaron shall lay both his hands on the head of the goat, and confess over it all the iniquities of the people of Israel, and all their transgressions, all their sins, putting them on the head of the goat, and sending it away into the wilderness. The goat shall bear on itself all their iniquities to a barren region; and the goat shall be set free in the wilderness.*[2]

The priest transferred the nation's sins to the goat when he laid his hands upon its head. The "scape-goat" then carried the

---

[1] Lev 17:10-11 (my bolding). Cf. Deut 12:23-25.
[2] Lev 16:21-22

sins far off into the desert. The whole ritual was based on psychological projection, of course, but nothing was known about that in those days.

# The Sacrifice of Christ

Belief in Christ's atonement for sin is nearly as old as belief in his resurrection. In the passage cited earlier from First Corinthians, Paul spoke of the fundamental importance of both:

*For I handed on to you as of first importance, what I in turn had received: that Christ died for our sins in accordance with the scriptures, and that he was buried, and that he was raised on the third day in accordance with the scriptures.*[1]

This was the beating heart of oral tradition, a chain that lengthened link by link by word of mouth before the gospels were written. Paul was a link in that long chain, passing along what others had told him.[2]

The New Testament is eminently clear about Jesus' death being a sacrifice for sin. **Romans** declares:

*All have sinned and fall short of the glory of God, but they are now justified by his grace as a gift, through the redemption that is in Christ Jesus, whom God put forward as a sacrifice of atonement by his blood. . . .*[3]

**Ephesians** repeats that thought:

*In him we have redemption through his blood, the forgiveness of our trespasses, according to the riches of his grace.*[4]

Gentiles at Ephesus were told:

---

[1] 1 Cor 15:3-4.
[2] Paul said otherwise, however, in Galatians (1:11-12):
   *I did not receive* (the gospel) *from a human source, nor was I taught it, but I received it through a revelation of Jesus Christ.*
[3] Rom 3:23-25a.
[4] Eph 1:7.

*now in Christ Jesus you who once were far off have been brought near by the blood of Christ.*[1]

**Colossians** declares that the whole universe was reconciled to God through Christ's blood:

*For in him all the fullness of God was pleased to dwell, and through him God was pleased to reconcile to himself all things, whether on earth or in heaven, by making peace through the blood of his cross.*[2]

**First Peter** talks of being "sprinkled with his blood."[3]

**First John** emphasizes truthfulness as a prerequisite for being cleansed by Jesus' blood:

*If we say that we have fellowship with him while we are walking in darkness, we lie and do not do what is true; but if we walk in the light as he himself is in the light, we have fellowship with one another, and the blood of Jesus his Son cleanses us from all sin.*[4]

The **Book of Revelation** was ascribed "To him who loves us and freed us from our sins by his blood."[5] Saints sing in heaven to the "Lamb that was slain":

*You are worthy to take the scroll and to open its seals, for you were slaughtered and by your blood you ransomed for God saints from every tribe and language and people and nation.*[6]

Martyrs are said to "have come out of the great ordeal; they have washed their robes and made them white in the blood of the Lamb,"[7] which ultimately defeats the devil himself.[8]

---

[1] Eph 2:13.
[2] Col 1:19-20.
[3] 1 Pet 1:2b.
[4] 1 John 1:6-7.
[5] Rev 1:5b.
[6] Rev 5:9; cf 5:12.
[7] Rev 7:14b.
[8] Rev 12:11a.

**Hebrews** says more about the blood of Christ than any other book in the New Testament. It was written by a Jew who believed in Christ, and pictured him as "a merciful and faithful high priest in the service of God, to make a sacrifice of atonement for the sins of the people."[1]

Contracts were ratified by blood:[2]

*Hence not even the first covenant was inaugurated without blood. For when every commandment had been told to all the people by Moses in accordance with the law, he took the blood of calves and goats, with water and scarlet wool and hyssop, and sprinkled both the scroll itself and all the people, saying, "This is the blood of the covenant that God has ordained for you." And in the same way he sprinkled with the blood both the tent and all the vessels used in worship. Indeed, under the law almost everything is purified with blood, and without the shedding of blood there is no forgiveness of sins.[3]*

However, since "it is impossible for the blood of bulls and goats to take away sins,"[4] the covenant with Moses was flawed from the start. That's why a new covenant, sealed by the blood of Christ, was needed:

*But when Christ came as a high priest of the good things that have come . . . he entered once for all into the Holy Place, not with the blood of goats and calves, but with his own blood, thus obtaining eternal redemption. For if the blood of goats and bulls, with the sprinkling of the ashes of a heifer, sanctifies those who have been defiled so that their flesh is purified, how much more will the blood of Christ, who through the eternal Spirit offered himself*

---

[1] Heb 2:16b-17; cf Heb 3:1-6; 4:14-15; 5:1-10; 6:19-20; 7:11-28.
[2] As seen in Gen 15:7-20.
[3] Heb 9:18-22.
[4] Heb 10:4.

*with out blemish to God, purify our conscience from dead works to worship the living God!* [1]

Even when not mentioned, Jesus' blood is always presupposed in passages that speak of atoning for sin.[2]

# The Mythological Presuppositions of Atonement

The concept of atonement is rooted in ancient Near Eastern mythology. The presuppositions behind the idea can be traced to two myths in particular, one of which describes a garden and the other a flood.

These myths arose in the bronze age, if not earlier. They appear in Genesis because Israel shared a common culture with other countries in the ancient near east.

The bible was pivotal in defining western civilization, and these myths express views of God and human nature that became normative in western society. Both portray humans as sinful, and God as being angry at them for sinning. These are the presuppositions that undergird the dogma of Christ's atonement.

## The Garden of Eden

The myth of the Garden of Eden envisions a perfect world.[3] A man and woman till a bountiful garden that meets their every need. All was well until a talking snake tricked the woman into eating fruit that God had forbidden them to eat. She in turn enticed the man to eat it. The consequences of their disobedience

---

[1] Heb 9:11-14. See also Heb 10:19-22.

[2] Galatians (1:3-4), for instance, opens with the words: *"Grace to you and peace from God our Father and the Lord Jesus Christ, who gave himself for our sins to set us free from the present evil age, according to the will of our God and Father."*

An example from Second Corinthians (5:21) alludes to the goat for Azazael: *"For our sake he made him to be sin who knew no sin, so that in him we might become the righteousness of God."*

[3] Gen 2:4b-14 and 2:15-3:24 are separate accounts of the garden.

were disastrous. Expelled from Eden, they found themselves living in misery. Childbirth was painful. Thorns and weeds choked their crops. Suffering and the prospect of death sha-dowed them. Their carefree life in paradise was gone—and all for a bite of fruit! Their relationship to God, and that of their descendants, was destroyed forever. As the first man and wo-man on earth, their "original sin" spread like a virus throughout the whole human race.

This myth explained the origin of suffering. In comparing Jesus to Adam, Paul took it literally:

> *Therefore just as one man's trespass led to condemnation for all, so one man's act of righteousness leads to justification and life for all. For just as by the one man's disobedience the many were made sinners, so by the one man's obedience the many will be made righteous.*[1]

Sixteen centuries later, Puritan children in New England re-cited the jingle, "In Adam's fall, we sinned all."[2] Incredibly, even today, some people still think the Garden of Eden really existed and blame poor old Adam for all the world's woes!

## The Deluge

The second myth was a Mesopotamian story called the Gil-gamesh Epic, which described a great flood covering the earth. It tells how the god Enki instructed a man named Utnapishtim to build a boat called the "Preserver of Life" prior to a flood that would drown all life on earth. The biblical version of the myth replaces Utnapishtim with Noah, but otherwise repeats the Mesopotamian story.

Genesis explains why God flooded the earth:

> *The Lord saw that the wickedness of humankind was great in the earth, and that every inclination of the thoughts of their hearts was only evil continually. And the Lord was sorry*

---

[1] Rom 5:18-19.
[2] New England Primer of 1677.

*that he had made humankind on the earth, and it grieved him
to his heart. So the Lord said, "I will blot out from the earth
the human beings I have created—people together with animals and creeping things and birds of the air, for I am sorry
that I have made them."*[1]

"Every inclination of the thoughts of their hearts was only
evil continually." The Hebrew text is harsh and pointed: *raq ra*[c]
(רק רע)—"only evil continually." That idea resurfaced during
the Protestant Reformation in the Calvinist doctrine of "total depravity," which declared that humans, by nature, are completely
corrupt.[2]

## Sin and the Wrath of God

The doctrine of Christ's atonement presupposes human sin-
fulness, and a god angry at humans for sinning. That's crystal
clear from this passage in **Romans**:

*But God proves his love for us in that while we still were sin-
ners Christ died for us. Much more surely then, now that we
have been justified by his blood, will we be saved through
him from the wrath of God.*[3]

Think about this for a moment. Christ's gruesome death per-
suaded God to forgive us? He isn't mad anymore? Now he
loves us? All because Christ died on a cross? How does that
differ from any other sacrifice in the ancient world? The god
Paul described belongs to that age. Animals aren't sacrificed
to angry gods these days. Yet, whenever Christians say Christ
died for their sins, they unwittingly replicate that primitive

---

[1] Gen 6:5-7.

[2] ". . . original sin is seen to be an hereditary depravity and corruption of our
nature, diffused into all parts of the soul. . . . Whatever is in man, from intel-
lect to will, from the soul to the flesh, is all defiled and crammed with concu-
piscence (the impulse to sin)." John Calvin, *The Institutes of the Christian
Church*, 1559 (Weber, *The Western Tradition*, 44).

[3] Rom 5:8-9.

ritual in their minds. Contrary to Jonathan Edwards' belief, we aren't "Sinners in the Hands of an Angry God."[1]

Christ's agonizing death proves God's love? What nonsense! We don't kill the ones we love. The idea of Christ's death buying God's love is utterly repugnant. Love isn't transactional. It isn't a *quid pro quo*, exchanging something for something else, or a matter of *do ut des*, giving in order to get. Love is selfless. It's freely given with no thought of getting anything in return. But that's not what we see in Romans. The god portrayed above was no different from any other god in antiquity who had to be pacified by killing an animal. But that's not love. It's a caricature of love.[2]

The "Penitential Prayer to Every God" suggests that guilt produces angst. Guilt buried in our subconscious mind demands punishment, which we unconsciously inflict upon ourselves in various ways from drug and alcohol abuse to self-mutilation and suicide. Imagining God is angry at us is another way of punishing ourselves, but it's nothing more than the projection of our own guilt upon God.

# Why was Jesus' Death considered a Sacrifice?

Jews from across the Roman Empire came to Jerusalem for Passover. The city's population doubled or tripled at Passover and might even have reached a hundred thousand people.[3] An

---

[1] Jonathan Edwards (1703-58) was a leading figure in the first Great Awakening in America. "Sinners in the Hands of an Angry God" was his most famous sermon.

[2] Despite his depiction of God in Romans, Paul was well aware of what genuine love was like:

> Love is patient; love is kind; love is not envious or boastful or arrogant or rude. It does not insist on its own way; it is not irritable or resentful; it does not rejoice in wrongdoing, but rejoices in the truth. It bears all things, believes all things, hopes all things, endures all things. (1 Cor 13:4-7)

[3] Joachim Jeremias, *Jerusalem in the time of Jesus, An Investigation into Economic and Social Conditions during the New Testament Period* (trans. F. H. and C. H. Cave; Philadelphia: Fortress Press, 1975), 84.

estimated eighteen thousand lambs were slain on the day of Passover for the meal that evening.[1]  Slaughtering began around three in the afternoon with three blasts from a *shophar* (ram's horn).[2]

The synoptic gospels of Mark, Matthew and Luke agree that Jesus died as the slaughtering began:[3]

*When it was noon, darkness came over the whole land until three in the afternoon. At three o'clock Jesus cried out with a loud voice, "Eloi, Eloi, lema sabachthani?" which means, "My God, my God, why have you forsaken me?" .... Then Jesus gave a loud cry and breathed his last.*[4]

Jesus' death at that time of the afternoon was seen as no coincidence.  Like the lambs being slaughtered, he too was slain for the sins of the people.  His blood, like the blood of innocent lambs, atoned for their sins.  Associating Jesus' death on the cross with the slaughtering of lambs at that hour couldn't have been more natural.

# The "Lamb of God"

Jesus was often called the "Lamb of God."  The **Gospel of John** says that, on seeing Jesus, John the Baptist said, "Here is the Lamb of God who takes away the sin of the  world!"[5]

The **Acts of the Apostles** tells the story of an Ethiopian official reading Isaiah on his way home, and coming across the passage that says, "Like a sheep he was led to slaughter."[1]  He was mystified by those words, and as he pondered what they might

---

[1] Jeremias, *Jerusalem*, 82.
[2] J. C. Rylaarsdam, "Passover" in *The Interpreter's Dictionary of the Bible* (ed. George Arthur Buttrick; Nashville: Abingdon, 1962), 665.
[3] Their agreement on this point (Mark 14:12-16; Matt 26:17-19; Luke 22:7-13) means that the last supper was *not* a Passover meal.  John's dating of the last supper (John 13:1) to the evening of the day *before* Passover is thus correct.
[4] Mark 15:33-34, 37; Matt 27:45-46, 50; Luke 23:44-46.
[5] John 1:29.

mean, the apostle Philip appeared, "And starting with this scripture, he proclaimed to him the good news about Jesus." Christians assumed Isaiah had Jesus in mind, and used these words to bolster their claim that Christ died for the sins of the world.[1]

**First Corinthians** states, "For our paschal lamb, Christ, has been sacrificed."[2]

**First Peter** draws the same comparison:

*You know that you were ransomed from the futile ways inherited from your ancestors, not with perishable things like silver or gold, but with the precious blood of Christ, like that of a lamb without defect or blemish.*[3]

The Book of **Revelation** alone contains twenty-nine references to Jesus as the Lamb of God.[4] These and the passages above establish a clear link between Jesus' death and the slaughter of lambs at Passover.

# Summary

To speak of Jesus' death as "propitiating" God or "expiating" sin calls an old gospel song to mind: "There is a fountain filled with blood drawn from Emmanuel's veins, and sinners plunged beneath that flood lose all their guilty stains." This stanza evokes feelings not unlike those felt by ancient people as they watched the throats of sacrificial animals being slit.

**Of all the dogmas of the church, none is more anachronistic in today's world than that of the atonement.** Jesus didn't die for the sins of the world. He died as a threat to Roman rule in Palestine.

---

[1] Isa 52:13-53:12.
[2] 1 Cor 5:7b.
[3] 1 Pet 1:18-19.
[4] Rev 5:6,8,12,13; 6:1,16; 7:9,10,14,17; 8:1; 12:11; 13:8,11; 14:1,4,10; 15:3; 17:14; 19:7,9; 21:9,14,22,23; 22:1,3.

# PART TWO
# LATER DOGMAS

# Chapter Three
## SECOND COMING

The first Christians expected Jesus to return to earth while they were still alive. They thought he would descend from heaven in power and glory, overthrow the evil kingdoms of the world and inaugurate a new age of universal peace. People on earth would acknowledge him as Lord of all on that day, and the ignominy of his death on a cross would be forgotten. This cosmic event, called the "**Parousia**," was eagerly awaited.

Christians were all the more eager for Jesus to return when they were being persecuted. Their suffering would be over on the day he appeared:

*For it is indeed just of God to repay with affliction those who afflict you, and to give relief to the afflicted as well as to us, when the Lord Jesus is revealed from heaven with his mighty angels in flaming fire, inflicting vengeance on those who do not know God and on those who do not obey the gospel of our Lord Jesus. These will suffer the punishment of eternal destruction, separated from the presence of the Lord and from the glory of his might, when he comes to be glorified by his saints and to be marveled at on that day among all who have believed.*[1]

The cosmos would be rehabilitated on the day Jesus returned. Creation itself would be recreated, "set free from its bondage to decay,"[2] and Christians would see their bodies transformed:

*I consider that the sufferings of this present time are not worth comparing with the glory about to be revealed to us. For the creation waits with eager longing for the revealing of the children of God . . . . We know that the whole creation*

---

[1] 2 Thess 1:6-10.
[2] Rom 8:21a.

*has been groaning in labor pains until now; and not only the creation, but we ourselves, who have the first fruits of the Spirit, groan inwardly while we wait for adoption, the redemption of our bodies.*[1]

The **Book of Revelation** was written a decade or two after a purge by the Roman Emperor Domitian in 81 CE.[2] Christians were being executed in Asia Minor, and the fantastic imagery in the book was meant to strengthen them in the face of death.[3] It begins with an affirmation and a blessing:

*The revelation of Jesus Christ, which God gave him to show his servants what must soon take place. . . . Blessed is the one who reads aloud the words of the prophecy, and blessed are those who hear and who keep what is written in it; for the time is near.*[4]

A series of phantasmagorical visions follows, and readers are told, "Do not seal up the words of the prophecy of this book, for the time is near."[5] The book closes with a promise, "Surely I am coming soon," and a fervent response, "Amen. Come, Lord Jesus!"[6]

## The Imminence of Jesus' Return

The striking thing about this belief is that early Christians expected Jesus to return to earth *while they were still alive.* Paul was sure that he and the Christians to whom he wrote would live to see Jesus on earth again. **First Thessalonians**, his oldest surviving letter,[7] makes that clear:

---

[1] Rom 8:18-19, 22-23.
[2] Kümmel, *Introduction*, 469.
[3] The Revelation to John wasn't written for us. It doesn't predict an apocalypse in our time. It was written for Christians being martyred two thousand years ago, who prayed for Jesus to come down from heaven and save them. That the world still endures would have been inconceivable to them.
[4] Rev 1:1,3.
[5] Rev 22:10.
[6] Rev 22:20.
[7] The letter was written around 50 CE (Kümmel, *Introduction*, 257).

*For what is our hope or joy or crown of boasting before our Lord Jesus at his coming?  **Is it not you?**[1]*

The Thessalonians themselves were living proof of Paul's faithfulness to God, and thus urged to be "blameless before our God and Father at the coming of our Lord Jesus with all his saints."[2]  Some might not live long enough to see Jesus on earth, but they would surely meet him in heaven.  Living and dead alike would rise to meet him in the sky on the day he returned:

*For the Lord himself, with a cry of command, with the arch-angel's call and the sound of God's trumpet, will descend from heaven, and the dead in Christ will rise first.  Then we who are alive, who are left, will be caught up in the clouds together with them to meet the Lord in the air; and so we will be with the Lord forever.[3]*

Paul ended with the words, "May your spirit and soul and body be kept sound and blameless at the coming of our Lord Jesus Christ."[4]

Believers at **Corinth** were comforted by hearing, "You are not lacking in any spiritual gift as you wait for the revealing of our Lord Jesus Christ."[5]

The **Phillipians** were also prepared to meet Christ:

*I am confident of this, that the one who began a good work among you will bring it to completion by the day of Jesus Christ.[6]*

Paul prayed for their love to grow, "so that in the day of Christ you may be pure and blameless."[7]  They, like the

---

[1] 1 Thess 2:19 (my bolding).

[2] 1 Thess 3:13.

[3] 1 Thess 4:16-17.

[4] 1 Thess 5:23.

[5] 1 Cor 1:7.

[6] Phil 1:6.

[7] Phil 1:10.

Christians at Thessalonica, served as living proof of his own faithfulness to Christ:

*It is by your holding fast to the word of life that I can boast on the day of Christ that I did not run in vain or labor in vain.*[1]

Paul warned against self-indulgence and immorality because "our citizenship is in heaven, and it is from there that we are expecting a Savior, the Lord Jesus Christ."[2] The letter closes by saying, "The Lord is near."[3]

The **Colossians** were told: "When Christ who is your life is revealed, then you also will be revealed with him in glory."[4]

**Paul's words show that he and other first-generation Christians expected Jesus to reappear during their lifetime.**

In fact, they thought he might show up at any moment! Paul urged everyone to be vigilant because Jesus would come "like a thief in the night":[5]

*For you yourselves know very well that the day of the Lord will come like a thief in the night. When they say, 'There is peace and security,' then sudden destruction will come upon them, as labor pains come upon a pregnant woman, and there will be no escape!*[6]

The expectation of Jesus' imminent return was so strong that some believers stopped working![7] After all, if Jesus might come back at any moment, why bother to work?

---

[1] Phil 2:16.
[2] Phil 3:20.
[3] Phil 4:5b.
[4] Col 3:4.
[5] This simile often appears in the New Testament (e.g. Matt 24:42-44; Luke 12:39-40; 1 Thess 5:2,4: 2 Pet 3:10; Rev 3:3, 16:15).
[6] 1 Thess 5:2-3.
[7] 2 Thess 3:11.

Paul advised against making any major changes in one's life:

*I think that, in view of the impending crisis, it is well for you to remain as you are. Are you bound to a wife? Do not seek to be free. Are you free from a wife? Do not seek a wife . . . I mean, brothers and sisters, the appointed time has grown short; from now on, let even those who have wives be as though they had none, and those who mourn as though they were not mourning, and those who rejoice as though they were not rejoicing, and those who buy as though they had no possessions, and those who deal with the world as though they had no dealings with it. For the present form of this world is passing away.*[1]

An Aramaic prayer passed down through oral tradition captured the intensity of this hope. *Maran atha*—Our Lord, come!"—was uttered in the fervent hope of speeding Jesus' return.[2]

The Eucharist itself was celebrated in the hope of hastening his return:

*For as often as you eat this bread and drink the cup, you proclaim the Lord's death until he comes.*[3]

## Delay of the Parousia

Although Jesus was expected at any time, Paul warned his readers not to get too excited about it:

*As to the coming of our Lord Jesus Christ and our being gathered together to him, we beg you, brothers and sisters, not to be quickly shaken in mind or alarmed, either by spirit or by word or by letter, as though from us, to the effect that the day of the Lord is already here.*[4]

---

[1] 1 Cor 7:26-31.
[2] 1 Cor 16:22. The same prayer, in Greek, appears at the end of the Revelation to John (22:20).
[3] 1 Cor 11:26.
[4] 2 Thess 2:1-2.

Paul told Christians who left their jobs to get back to work. Freeloading wasn't tolerated: "Anyone unwilling to work should not eat." Everyone was expected "to do their work quietly and to earn their own living."[1] Their responsibilities here on earth were more important than looking up at the sky.

Paul was bothered by Jesus' continued failure to appear and rationalized it by saying Jesus was waiting for Satan to start a worldwide rebellion against God before he returned.[2] Moreover, seen from a positive angle, the ongoing delay allowed more time for people to be saved![3]

Nevertheless, as time kept passing with no sign of Jesus, Christians started asking if he was ever going to return. First-generation Christians were dying, along with their hope of seeing Jesus come back to earth. Nevertheless, Paul was steadfast. He was sure that everyone, living or dead, would see Jesus before long:

> *Listen, I will tell you a mystery! We will not all die, but we will all be changed, in a moment, in the twinkling of an eye, at the last trumpet. For the trumpet will sound, and the dead will be raised imperishable, and we will be changed.*[4]

In the meantime, Paul focused on the bond that bound Christians to Christ here and now. No matter what they suffered, their risen Lord was always beside them:

> *Who will separate us from the love of Christ? Will hardship, or distress, or persecution, or famine, or nakedness, or peril, or sword? As it is written,*
> *   "For your sake we are being killed all day long;*
> *   We are accounted as sheep to be slaughtered."*
> *No, in all these things we are more than conquerors through him who loved us. For I am convinced that neither death,*

---

[1] 2 Thess 3:10b,12.
[2] 2 Thess 2:3.
[3] Rom 2:4.
[4] 1 Cor 15:51-52.

*nor life, nor angels, nor rulers, nor things present, nor
things to come, nor powers, nor height, nor depth, nor anything else in all creation, will be able to separate us from the
love of God in Christ Jesus our Lord.* [1]

The bond between Christians and their risen Lord gradually superseded the hope of seeing Jesus on earth again. Christians didn't have to wait for him to return because he was already with them, here and now, every moment of their lives:

*We do not live to ourselves, and we do not die to ourselves.
If we live, we live to the Lord, and if we die, we die to the
Lord; so then, whether we live or whether we die, we are
the Lord's.* [2]

Comparing Paul's letters to the gospels shows how hope for Jesus' return had faded by the end of the first century. Paul's letters were written in the early fifties of the first century. The first written gospel, the Gospel of Mark, appeared over a generation later, and the gospels of Matthew and Luke appeared a decade or so after Mark. Paul's letters are filled with references to Jesus' return, but the first three gospels barely mention it. Mark has three references to Jesus' return. [3] Matthew and Luke repeat Mark's three references, [4] and Matthew adds a fourth that doesn't appear in Mark or Luke. [5] Only four independent references to Jesus' return appear in these three gospels. As compared to Paul's letters, the scarcity of these references reveals how steeply interest in Jesus' return declined between the middle and end of the first century.

The Gospel of John doesn't mention returning to earth, but speaks instead of the coming of the Holy Spirit. [6] John was the

---

[1] Rom 8:35-39.
[2] Rom 14:7-8.
[3] Mark 9:1, 13:30, and 14:62.
[4] Mark 9:1 = Matt 16:28 and Luke 9:27. Mark 13:30 = Matt 24:34 and Luke 21:32. Mark 14:62 = Matt 26:64 and Luke 22:69.
[5] Matt 10:23.
[6] John 7:39; 14:16, 26; 15:26; 16:13 and 20:22.

45

last gospel written, and the fact that Jesus' return to earth isn't even mentioned is further evidence of that hope being lost.

Opinions varied at the end of the first century about Jesus' return to earth. Comparing two documents written at the same approximate time and attributed to the same Apostle makes that evident. The *Gospel* of John and the *Revelation* to John were written around the end of the first century[1] and pseudonymously attributed to the Apostle John. The views they ascribe to him, however, are at opposite ends of the spectrum. The Gospel of John doesn't mention Jesus' return to earth, whereas the Revelation to John emphasizes it! The contrast between documents written in the same timeframe and ascribed to the same Apostle highlights the variety of opinions held at the close of the first century about Jesus' return to earth.

The **Letter to the Hebrews** is torn between hope for Jesus' return and the reality of his failure to appear. Written in the eighth decade of the first century,[2] it states that:

*Christ, having been offered once to bear the sins of many, will appear a second time, not to deal with sin, but to save those who are eagerly waiting for him.*[3]

The letter avows that "in a very little while, the one who is coming will come and will not delay."[4] However, by the time Hebrews was written, that hope was fading and all but lost.

The author was hard-pressed to show that Jesus was still going to return. He began by reminding his readers of the great heroes of the past:

*Who through faith conquered kingdoms, administered jus tice, obtained promises, shut the mouths of lions, quenched raging fire, escaped the edge of the sword, won strength out of weakness, became mighty in war, put foreign armies to*

---

[1] Kümmel, *Introduction*, 246, 469.
[2] Kümmel, *Introduction*, 403.
[3] Heb 9:28.
[4] Heb 10:37.

*flight . . . . Others suffered mocking and flogging, and even chains and imprisonment. They were stoned to death, they were sawn in two, they were killed by the sword; they went about in skins of sheep and goats, destitute, persecuted, tormented—of whom the world was not worthy.*[1]

These examples reminded the letter's recipients that many others before them had also suffered for their faith. Being persecuted qualified them to join the ranks of those exalted martyrs.

The writer then turned to Jesus:

*Therefore, since we are surrounded by so great a cloud of witnesses, let us also lay aside every weight and the sin that clings so closely, and let us run with perseverance the race that is set before us, looking to Jesus the pioneer and perfecter of our faith, who for the sake of the joy that was set before him endured the cross, disregarding its shame, and has taken his seat at the right hand of the throne of God.*[2]

Rightly seen, persecution was a form of discipline:

*My child, do not regard lightly the discipline of the Lord, or lose heart when you are punished by him; for the Lord disciplines those whom he loves, and chastises every child whom he accepts.*[3]

So, there you have it. Persecution proves God's love! It purifies faith like a refiner's fire, develops strength of character and puts steel in one's spine:

*Now, discipline always seems painful rather than pleasant at the time, but later it yields the peaceful fruit of righteousness to those who have been trained by it.*[4]

---

[1] Heb 11:33-38.
[2] Heb 12:1-2.
[3] Heb 12:5-6 (quoting Prov 3:11-12).
[4] Heb 12:11.

Understood as discipline, persecution was nothing to fear. In fact, it made them better Christians!

The letter ends with a promise. If its readers didn't live to see Jesus come back to earth, they would surely meet him in heaven:

*You have not come to something that can be touched . . .*
*But you have come to Mount Zion and to the city of the living*
*God, the heavenly Jerusalem, and to innumerable angels in*
*festal gathering, and to the assembly of the firstborn who are*
*enrolled in heaven, and to God the judge of all, and to the*
*spirits of the righteous made perfect, and to Jesus . . . .*
*For here we have no lasting city, but we are looking for the*
*city that is to come.*[1]

Nevertheless, as time rolled on, believing in Jesus' return to earth became increasingly difficult. The **Letter of James**, written around the end of the first century,[2] pleads for patience and reiterates the old hope:

*Be patient, beloved, until the coming of the Lord. The far-*
*mer waits for the precious crop from the earth, being patient*
*with it until it receives the early and the late rains. You also*
*must be patient. Strengthen your hearts, for the coming of*
*the Lord is near.*[3]

Four or five decades later,[4] the person who wrote **Second Peter** confronted outright cynicism:

*First of all you must understand this, that in the last days*
*scoffers will come, scoffing and indulging their own lusts*
*and saying, "Where is the promise of his coming? For ever*
*since our ancestors died, all things continue as they were*
*from the beginning of creation!"*[5]

---

[1] Heb 12:18; 12:22-23; 13:14.

[2] Kümmel, *Introduction*, 414.

[3] Jas 5:7-8

[4] Kümmel, *Introduction*, 434 (125-150 CE?).

[5] 2 Pet 3:3-4.

The author cautioned his readers against thinking of Christ's return in human terms:

> *But do not ignore this one fact, beloved, that with the Lord one day is like a thousand years, and a thousand years are like one day. The Lord is not slow about his promise, as some think of slowness, but is patient with you, not wanting any to perish, but all to come to repentance. But the day of the Lord will come like a thief, and then the heavens will pass away with a loud noise, and the elements will be dissolved with fire, and the earth and everything that is done on it will be burned up.*[1]

The arguments are forced: God has his own time-table; time is meaningless in relation to eternity; Christ's delay allows more time for people to repent. The writer ended with a fear tactic: believe in Christ's return—or you'll be burned to a crisp when he shows up!

## The Church's Crisis of Faith

Jesus' failure to appear created a crisis of faith in the early church. Christians couldn't understand why he hadn't come back. Where was the promise of God's kingdom on earth? Tyrants still ruled the world. Suffering and death continued unabated. The sun rose and set each day as always. Nothing had changed and people dragged along their old weary ways. The pro-verb, "Hope deferred makes the heart sick"[2] was right. So, as life in the old age ground on, hope for a new age crumbled.

But another took its place. The hope of seeing Jesus on earth gave way to the hope of meeting him in heaven. After all, there was no reason for him to return. What would he gain? He was in heaven seated on a glorious throne next to almighty God himself. What more could he want? So, why leave? Besides that, this age was passing away. Life on earth was preparation for

---

[1] 2 Pet 3:8-10 (v. 10 alternate reading).
[2] Prov 13:12a.

49

heaven. Injustice and oppression were hard to bear, but they wouldn't last. Eternal life with Christ was all that mattered.

Moreover, Christians had to get on with their lives. They had work to do and families to raise. Expecting Jesus to reappear on earth distracted them from the business of living. So it was inevitable. The hope of seeing Jesus on earth gradually faded away. But it wasn't discarded. It became a relic of the past, preserved in creeds and baptismal formulas with no relevance to Christians' everyday lives.

Having said all this, one might ask how the idea of Christ's returning to earth arose in the first place. Why did early Christians expect him to descend from heaven? The answer lies in the Book of Daniel:

> *I saw in the night visions, and behold, with the clouds of heaven there came one like a son of man, and he came to the Ancient of Days and was presented before him. And to him was given dominion and glory and kingdom, that all peoples, nations, and languages should serve him; his dominion is an everlasting dominion, which shall not pass away, and his kingdom one that shall not be destroyed.* [1]

Jesus' expectation of God's heavenly kingdom descending to earth was based on this prophecy. The appearance of Daniel's "son of man" in the sky would signal the start of an apocalypse that would put an end to this evil age and inaugurate a new age of world peace ruled by God.

But Daniel's "son of man" never appeared, and hope for God's kingdom coming to earth died on the cross with Jesus. But that didn't end the matter. Daniel's mysterious "son of man" coming on the clouds of heaven was identified as Jesus, the "Son of Man." Having risen to heaven, he could now descend from heaven. So, by virtue of his resurrection and

---

[1] Dan 7:13-14 (RSV). A "son of man" simply meant a "human being."

exaltation, Jesus' expectation of "a son of man" was transferred to Jesus himself.

The historical Jesus, however, never called himself the "Son of Man."[1] He *expected* a "son of man," a cosmic figure appearing in the sky, but never claimed to *be* that figure—despite being seen as such by his followers after he died.

---

[1] This is discussed in depth in my next book, *A FATAL MISTAKE: Jesus and the Kingdom that Never Came.*

# Chapter Four
## PREEXISTENCE; INCARNATION; VIRGIN BIRTH; ASCENSION

These dogmas are grouped together because they belong to a mythical cycle of leaving and returning to heaven.

## Preexistence

Early Christians had no difficulty worshipping Jesus as a god because their world was filled with "many gods and many lords."[1] Gods competed against other gods in the ancient world. That's why Jesus had to become one. Christians would have been at a competitive disadvantage vis-à-vis the other religions of the day if Jesus had merely been a man. Making him a god leveled the playing field.

By rising from the dead, Jesus proved that he, too, was a god. Gods by definition are immortal, with no beginning or end. Therefore, as a god, Jesus existed *before* he was born on earth.

### Belief in Jesus' Divinity

That belief found voice in an early hymn embedded in **Philippians**. Paul quoted the hymn to shame believers who were arrogant about having charismatic gifts. "Let the same mind be in you that was in Christ Jesus,"

> *who, though he was in the form of God,*
> *did not regard equality with God*
> *as something to be exploited but emptied himself,*
> *taking the form of a slave,*
> *being born in human likeness.*

---

[1] 1 Cor 8:5.

*And being found in human form, he humbled himself*
*and became obedient to the point of death—*
*even death on a cross.*
*Therefore God also highly exalted him*
*and gave him the name that is above every name,*
*so that at the name of Jesus every knee should bend,*
*in heaven and on earth and under the earth,*
*and every tongue should confess that Jesus Christ is Lord,*
*to the glory of God the Father.* [1]

This ancient hymn extols Jesus for leaving a life of glory in heaven for a humble existence here on earth.

The **Gospel of John** begins by echoing the opening verse of Genesis:

*In the beginning was the Word (**Logos**),*
*and the Word (**Logos**) was with God,*
*and the Word (**Logos**) was God.*
*He was in the beginning with God.*
*All things came into being through him,*
*and without him not one thing came into being*
*that has come into being.* [2]

The fourth gospel starts with the ***Logos***, the "Word" spoken by God in creating the universe. The *Logos* was God's *alter ego*—God in an alternate state of being. We'll discuss this in Part Three. We simply note here that *Jesus was identified as the Logos!* That's an astounding claim that went far beyond simple belief in his preexistence.

Jesus' role in creation is similarly emphasized in the **Letter to the Hebrews**:

*Long ago God spoke to our ancestors in many and various ways by the prophets, but in these last days he has spoken to us by a Son, whom he appointed heir of all things, through whom he also created the worlds. He is a reflection of*

---

[1] Phil 2:5-11. Mainstream scholars regard these verses as a primitive hymn.
[2] John 1:1-3 (alternate reading).

*God's glory and the exact imprint of God's very being, and he sustains all things by his powerful word.*[1]

The hymn of praise in Philippians, Jesus identified as the *Logos* in the Gospel of John, and this passage in Hebrews point to the ubiquity of early belief in Jesus' preexistence.

# Incarnation

Jesus' "incarnation" presupposed his preexistence. It marked the point at which he left eternity and entered the world of space and time. It was the portal through which he passed from one dimension to another. The Gospel of John expresses that idea in a single sentence: "And the Word became flesh and lived among us."[2] That was the moment of Christ's "incarnation." The term translates a Latin verb *(incarno)* that means "to make into flesh" or "to be made flesh," and expresses the belief that Christ, as a divine being, had to be "enfleshed" in order to enter our world. But that presented a problem. How could a *divine* being become a *human* being?[3] How was that possible? How could immortal spirit become mortal flesh?

# Virgin Birth

That question was answered by positing an intermediary between heaven and earth. A human mother, acting as a conduit, would enable the *Logos* to pass from eternity to time, "enfleshing" it through the process of gestation and allowing it to enter our world. But not just any mother. The *Logos* was pure, so the woman who bore it had to be pure herself.[4] If not, the purity of the *Logos* would be lost. A virgin, undefiled by sexual

---

[1] Hebrews 1:1-3a.

[2] John 1:14.

[3] This will be discussed at length in Chapter Six, which deals with the dogma of Christ's human and divine natures.

[4] The Roman Catholic doctrine of Mary's "Immaculate Conception" reflects this idea.

intercourse with a man, was the only woman qualified to bear the *Logos.*

# Matthew

The gospels of Matthew and Luke describe Mary as a virgin. The birth stories in each came from different streams of oral tradition ("M" in Matthew and "L" in Luke). Mary is pregnant in Matthew—but not with Joseph's child! When Joseph realizes she isn't carrying his child, he decides to break their engagement:

*Now the birth of Jesus the Messiah took place in this way. When his mother Mary had been engaged to Joseph, but before they lived together, she was found to be with child from the Holy Spirit. Her husband Joseph, being a righteous man and unwilling to expose her to public disgrace, planned to dismiss her quietly. But just when he had resolved to do this, an angel of the Lord appeared to him in a dream and said, "Joseph, son of David, do not be afraid to take Mary as your wife, for the child conceived in her is from the Holy Spirit. She will bear a son, and you are to name him Jesus, for he will save his people from their sins." All this took place to fulfill what had been spoken by the Lord through the prophet:*

*"Look, the virgin shall conceive and bear a son, and they shall name him Emmanuel," which means "God is with us."*

*When Joseph awoke from sleep, he did as the Angel of the Lord commanded him; he took her as his wife, but had no marital relations with her until she had borne a son; and he named him Jesus.*[1]

"Joseph, being a righteous man and unwilling to expose her to public disgrace, planned to dismiss her quietly." This means that Mary was pregnant with another man's child. Why else would Joseph have wanted to shield her from "public disgrace." What else explains his wanting to "dismiss her quietly." If the

---

[1] Matt 1:18-25 (citing Isaiah 7:14).

child were his, would he have turned his back on it? Would a "righteous man" do such a thing? No, if the child had been his, he wouldn't have wanted to cancel the wedding, and nothing would have been said about Mary's pregnancy. Claiming the child was conceived by the Holy Spirit was an attempt to avoid acknowledging that Joseph wasn't Jesus' father.

Suggesting that Jesus was illegitimate isn't farfetched. Rape has always been a weapon of war and Palestine was an occupied country. Laws governing the marriages of priests indicate that Jewish women were often raped by Roman soldiers. The laws were necessary because the legitimacy of a man's priesthood depended upon the purity of his genealogical line:

> Thus, not only was a priest forbidden to marry a woman who had been a prisoner of war, because she could not give him legitimate sons for the priesthood, but he could not continue to live with his wife if she had merely lived in a town occupied by the enemy, and could not prove her integrity by un prejudiced evidence. If he persisted in the marriage, it was regarded as concubinage and the children of the marriage were illegitimate.[1]

These restrictions presumed that female prisoners of war and women living in occupied towns had been raped, and were thus unfit to marry a priest.

Celsus, a second century critic of Christianity, asserted that Jesus' father was a Roman centurion named Panthera. Christians were viciously slandered at the beginning of the Common Era, and there's no way of knowing if this rumor were true. But one thing is certain: if Jesus was fathered by the Holy Spirit, he couldn't have been the son of a Roman soldier. The former precludes the latter. What better rebuttal could there have been?

---

[1] Jeremias, *Jerusalem*, 220.

56

# Isaiah's Prophecy

Matthew's story rests upon a prophecy from Isaiah: "Look, the virgin shall conceive and bear a son, and they shall name him Emmanuel."

In thinking about this, we need to realize that the bible wasn't written for us. It was written *by* ancient people *for* ancient people. This means that Isaiah's prophecy *wasn't* about Jesus. It concerned the birth of a child who was born seven centuries earlier than Jesus.

Isaiah's prophecy came at a critical moment in Israel's history.[1] Two neighboring kings were planning to attack Jerusalem, and its inhabitants were terrified. But not Isaiah. He foresaw the land being invaded by a mighty army that would sweep those petty kings away in its path. His prophecy would be confirmed by the impending birth of a boy named "Immanuel." The birth and naming of this child would certify to Jerusalem's king that, before the boy stopped breastfeeding, "the land before whose two kings you are in dread will be deserted."

So, "Immanuel" wasn't Jesus.[2] Immanuel was born seven centuries before Jesus came along.

# Luke

The annunciation story is different in Luke:

*In the sixth month the angel Gabriel was sent by God to a town in Galilee called Nazareth, to a virgin engaged to a man whose name was Joseph, of the house of David. The virgin's name was Mary. And he came to her and said, "Greetings, favored one! The Lord is with you." But she was much perplexed by his words and pondered what sort*

---

[1] Isa 7:1-17.

[2] Early Christians didn't know about historical accuracy. The Old Testament prophecies in Matthew (2:5,15,17,23; 3:3; 4:14; 8:17; 12:17; 13:35; 21:4; 26:56; 27:9) were ripped from their historical contexts and used to prove that Jesus was Israel's messiah.

*of greeting this might be. The angel said to her, "Do not be afraid, Mary, for you have found favor with God. And now, you will conceive in your womb and bear a son, and you will name him Jesus. He will be great and will be called the Son of the Most High, and the Lord God will give to him the throne of his ancestor David. He will reign over the house of Jacob forever, and of his kingdom there will be no end." Mary said to the angel, "How can this be, since I am a virgin?" The angel said to her, "The Holy Spirit will come upon you, and the power of the Most High will overshadow you; therefore the child to be born will be holy; he will be called Son of God."*[1]

Different stories are told in Matthew and Luke. Mary is pregnant in Matthew but not in Luke. She's told she'll *become* pregnant in Luke whereas in Matthew she's *already* pregnant. Christians were scandalized by the idea of Jesus' having been illegitimate, and asserted that Mary was a virgin to counteract that perception.

Nothing as salacious as Mary's liaison with another man would have been admitted if it weren't true. It was simply too embarrassing.[2] Matthew's account was based on its special source "M," which collected early Christian traditions. Mary's pregnancy could easily have been omitted from that source, and the fact that it wasn't speaks to the truth of Matthew's account. Luke, for its part, doesn't even mention Joseph, and Mary is said to be a virgin waiting to be impregnated by the Holy Spirit.

---

[1] Luke 1:26-35.

[2] Embarrassment as a testimony to the truth appears elsewhere in the New Testament. Jesus' baptism (Mk 1:9) by John the Baptist embarrassed Christians because it portrayed John as superior to Jesus (Matt 3:13-15 refutes that misperception). In like manner, Jesus' cry from the cross, "My God, my God, why have you forsaken me!" (Mark 15:34; Matt 27:46), mortified Christians because it admitted defeat. They were preserved nevertheless on account being his actual words.

One more point is relevant. The Greek text of Matthew calls Mary a "virgin" (*parthenos*), but that mistranslates "young woman" (*'almāh*) in Isaiah's prophecy. "Young woman" was a generic term used of any young woman, virgin or not. The mistranslation occurred when the Hebrew bible was being translated into Greek in the third and second centuries BCE. That translation, called the **Septuagint**, was the bible early Christians used,[1] which means that Old Testament passages quoted in the New came from the Septuagint, not the original Hebrew text—and that explains how a pregnant "young woman" in Isaiah became a "virgin" in Matthew.

Paul never mentioned Jesus' birth—let alone a virgin birth. He made a passing comment about Jesus' being "born of a woman,"[2] but that's all he ever said. His silence on this point, like his silence about an empty tomb, indicates that Peter, James and John, "the acknowledged leaders" of the church, never told him about a virgin birth when they met in Jerusalem,[3] which indicates in turn that they themselves hadn't heard of one.

The idea of Mary's virginity originated in oral tradition to counteract rumors of Jesus' illegitimacy and make the story of his birth more compelling.

# The Birth Stories

Mark and John say nothing about Jesus' birth.[4] Both gospels begin with John the Baptist, whose fiery apocalyptic message inspired Jesus' own preaching about the coming kingdom of God. Matthew and Luke, on the other hand, discuss Jesus' birth at length.[5] The stories they recount came from different streams

---

[1] The New Testament canon of twenty-seven scriptures wasn't set until the end of the fourth century CE.

[2] Gal 4:4.

[3] Gal 1:18-19, 2:1-2.

[4] Mark begins with John the Baptist and Jesus' ministry in Galilee (1:1-15). John begins with the preexistent *Logos*, and then moves to John the Baptist's ministry.

[5] Matt 1:18-2:12; Luke 2:1-20.

of oral tradition ("M" in Matthew and "L" in Luke).  Both are read together at Christmas as if they formed a single narrative.  But they don't.  Apart from depicting Mary as a virgin and Jesus as having been born in Bethlehem,[1] they have nothing in common.

# Matthew

Matthew reads as follows:

*In the time of King Herod, after Jesus was born in Bethlehem of Judea, wise men from the East came to Jerusalem, asking, "Where is the child who has been born king of the Jews?  For we observed his star at its rising, and have come to pay him homage."  When King Herod heard this, he was frightened, and all Jerusalem with him; and calling together all the chief priests and scribes of the people, he inquired of them where the Messiah was to be born.  They told him, "In Bethlehem of Judea; for so it has been written by the prophet:*

**'And you, Bethlehem, in the land of Judea, are by no means least among the rulers of Judah; for from you shall come a ruler who is to shepherd my people Israel.'"**

*Then Herod secretly called for the wise men and learned from them the exact time when the star had appeared.  Then he sent them to Bethlehem, saying, "Go and search diligently for the child; and when you have found him, bring me word so that I may also go and pay him homage."  When they had heard the king, they set out; and there, ahead of them, went the star that they had seen at its rising, until it stopped over the place where the child was.  When they saw that the star had stopped, they were overwhelmed with joy.  On entering the house, they saw the child with Mary his mother; and they knelt down and paid him homage.  Then, opening their treasure chests, they offered him gifts of gold, frankincense, and myrrh.  And having been warned in a*

---

[1] Jesus' supposed birth in Bethlehem was the starting point of both stories.  The idea arose in oral tradition and evolved along different lines.

*dream not to return to Herod, they left for their own country by another road.*

*Now after they had left, an angel of the Lord appeared to Joseph in a dream and said, "Get up, take the child and his mother, and flee to Egypt, and remain there until I tell you; for Herod is about to search for the child, to destroy him." Then Joseph got up, and took the child and his mother by night, and went to Egypt, and remained there until the death of Herod. This was to fulfill what had been spoken by the Lord through the prophet,*

**"Out of Egypt I have called my son."**

*When Herod saw that he had been tricked by the wise men, he was infuriated, and he sent and killed all the children in and around Bethlehem who were two years old or under, according to the time that he had learned from the wise men. Then was fulfilled what had been spoken through the prophet Jeremiah:*

**"A voice was heard in Ramah, wailing and loud lamentation, Rachel weeping for her children; she refused to be consoled, because they are no more."**

*When Herod died, an angel of the Lord suddenly appeared in a dream to Joseph in Egypt and said, "Get up, take the child and his mother, and go to the land of Israel, for those who were seeking the child's life are dead." Then Joseph got up, took the child and his mother, and went to the land of Israel. But when he heard that Archelaus was ruling over Judea in place of his father Herod, he was afraid to go there. And after being warned in a dream, he went away to the district of Galilee. There he made his home in a town called Nazareth, so that what had been spoken through the prophet might be fulfilled,*

**"He will be called a Nazorean."**[1]

---

[1] Matt 2:1-23.

Matthew represents Jesus' birth as the fulfillment of five Old Testament prophecies. The first involved the coming of "Immanuel." The next four dealt with the messiah's birthplace, the family's escape to Egypt, murdered children in Bethlehem, and Nazareth as the messiah's hometown. Matthew's author, himself a Jew, used these prophecies to persuade fellow Jews that Jesus was Israel's long-awaited messiah.[1]

But that was problematic. "Immanuel" was born seven centuries before Jesus. There's no record of Herod killing children in Bethlehem. Escaping to Egypt isn't confirmed anywhere else. The only prophecy that remotely applies to Jesus is the one about Nazareth being his hometown.

So, in light of these problems, why were they used? What purpose did they serve? It appears as if these prophecies served as *literary templates.* In other words, they weren't *fulfilled* by Jesus' birth; they were used to *describe it.* Nothing was known of Jesus' birth, and these prophecies filled that void by creating a fictional picture of it.[2]

Matthew's story of Jesus' birth is a tale of promises fulfilled, wise men and a wondrous star, innocent children murdered by a ruthless tyrant, homage paid to a newborn child and precious gifts laid at his feet. These were well known motifs in antiquity and easily adapted to a tale about Jesus' birth.[3] None of it was true, but it satisfied the curiosity of pious believers.

---

[1] Gentiles weren't concerned with Hebrew prophecy.

[2] As shown by the New Testament Apocrypha, wildly imaginative stories about Jesus' childhood were popular at the time, and this was one of them.

[3] The story of Jesus' birth continued to be embellished after Matthew was written. The magi became kings by the fifth century. Based on the gifts of gold, frankincense and myrrh, it was said that there were three. All had names—Kaspar, Balthasar and Melchior—by the eighth century, and Kaspar became a Moor in the fourteenth century. The elaboration of this story shows how easily it changed.

# Luke

The Gospel of Luke presents an entirely different picture:

*In those days a decree went out from Emperor Augustus that all the world should be registered. This was the first registration and was taken while Quirinius was governor of Syria. All went to their own towns to be registered. Joseph also went from the town of Nazareth in Galilee to Judea, to the city of David called Bethlehem, because he was descended from the house and family of David. He went to be registered with Mary, to whom he was engaged and who was expecting a child. While they were there, the time came for her to deliver her child. And she gave birth to her firstborn son and wrapped him in bands of cloth, and laid him in a manger, because there was no place for them in the inn.*

*In that region there were shepherds living in the fields, keeping watch over their flock by night. Then an angel of the Lord stood before them, and the glory of the Lord shone around them, and they were terrified. But the angel said to them, "Do not be afraid; for see—I am bringing you good news of great joy for all the people: to you is born this day in the city of David a Savior, who is the Messiah, the Lord. This will be a sign for you; you will find a child wrapped in bands of cloth and lying in a manger." And suddenly there was with the angel a multitude of the heavenly host, praising God and saying,*

*"Glory to God in the highest heaven,*
*and on earth peace among those whom he favors!"*

*When the angels had left them and gone into heaven, the shepherds said to one another, "Let us go now to Bethlehem and see this thing that has taken place, which the Lord has made known to us." So they went with haste and found Mary and Joseph, and the child lying in the manger. When they saw this, they made known what had been told them about this child; and all who heard it were amazed at what the shepherds told them. But Mary treasured all these words and pondered them in her heart. The shepherds returned, glorifying and praising God for all they had heard and seen, as it had been told them.*[1]

No Roman census took place in Syria at the time of Jesus' birth. Quirinius conducted one there in 6 CE, but that was a decade after Jesus was born.[2] This readjustment indicates that the census taken by Quirinius was backdated to the time of Jesus' birth. It was a literary device to get Mary and Joseph to Bethlehem in order to say Jesus was born there. An angel announcing his birth to shepherds and angels singing God's praise in heaven heightened the story's appeal.

A prologue precedes and an epilogue follows Jesus' birth in Luke. The prologue establishes a connection between John the Baptist and Jesus. John's mother Elizabeth is elderly, implying that his conception was as miraculous as Jesus' own conception. Mary, pregnant with Jesus, visits Elizabeth, who is pregnant with John. Elizabeth blesses Mary, and Mary in turn praises God for letting her bear the messiah.[3] The prologue ends with John's father Zechariah thanking God for giving his wife and him a child in their old age.[4]

The epilogue is set in the temple, where Joseph and Mary have gone to give thanks for their new baby boy. As they're doing so, they're approached by an elderly holy man who blesses God for letting him live long enough to see the messiah.[5] An aged prophetess follows, foretelling the child's future. Mary is amazed by what she hears (despite already having been told about it in the prologue!).[6]

---

[1] Luke 2:1-20.
[2] Scholars surmise that Jesus was born around 4-3 BCE.
[3] Her words come from an ancient Christian hymn called the "Magnificat."
[4] His words, known as the "Benedictus," also came from an ancient hymn.
[5] This is the "Nunc Dimittas" in the Roman Catholic Mass.
[6] This inconsistency indicates that Luke's special source "L," was itself composed of several strands of oral tradition.

The first two chapters in Luke focus on Jesus' birth. The material in both came from "L," the source found only in Luke. None of it is historical. It arose in oral tradition and is entirely fictional.

Apart from saying Mary was a virgin and Jesus was born in Bethlehem, the narratives in Matthew and Luke have nothing in common. Matthew doesn't mention a census under Caesar Augustus, a journey to Bethlehem, an inn or a manger or shepherds in the field or angels heralding Jesus' birth. Conversely, in Luke, nothing is said about Herod, or wise men from the East, or a guiding star, or children slaughtered in Bethlehem, or fleeing to Egypt. The stories are completely different, despite being read together at Christmas as parts of a single narrative.

# The Genealogies

The genealogies in Matthew and Luke beg an obvious question.[1] *If Jesus' father were God, how could he have had human ancestors?* The authors of Matthew and Luke apparently missed that contradiction, but others saw it. A later scribe came to the place that says, "Jesus was the son of Joseph," and caught the mistake. He knew that Jesus' father was God, not Joseph, and inserted a parenthetical comment to clarify the statement: *"*Jesus was the son *(as was thought)* of Joseph.*"*[2]

Like the stories of Jesus' birth, the genealogies in these gospels are fictional. Apart from a famous name or two in common, they list completely different ancestors for Jesus! This discrepancy is explained by their having arisen in separate streams of oral tradition. The "M" source in Matthew starts with Abraham and *ends* with Jesus, whereas the "L" source in Luke *begins* with Jesus and traces his ancestors all the way back to Adam! Both sources agree that Jesus' father was Joseph but starting with Jesus' grandfather (Jacob in Matthew; Heli in Luke), they go in completely different directions.

---

[1] Matt 1:1-16; Luke 3:23-38.
[2] Luke 3:23 (my italics).

One might ask why these exhaustive genealogies were compiled when they so obviously contradict the story of Jesus' conception by the Holy Spirit. The answer is found in the first century Jewish expectation of a messiah from the lineage of David. Convincing Jews that Jesus was Israel's messiah was made all the more difficult by that expectation.

For one simple reason: as shown by his own words, **Jesus didn't descend from David.**[1] Therefore, to prove Jesus was Israel's long-awaited messiah, the first Christians—all of whom were Jews—had to link him to David. That's why the birth stories and genealogies were written. The fictional birth stories connected him to Bethlehem, the "City of David," and the spurious genealogies established a blood relationship with David.

# Jesus' Birthplace

The Gospel of John says that being born in Nazareth was a problem:

*Some in the crowd said, "This is really the prophet." Others said, "This is the Messiah." But some asked, "Surely the Messiah does not come from Galilee, does he? Has not the scripture said that the Messiah is descended from David and comes from Bethlehem, the village where David lived?"*[2]

The messiah was supposed to come from Bethlehem, not Nazareth. Nazareth was located in the hill country of Galilee, a hundred miles north of Bethlehem. When a prospective disciple was told, "We have found him about whom Moses in the law and also the prophets wrote, Jesus son of Joseph from Nazareth," he scornfully replied, "Can anything good come out of

---

[1] Mark 12:35-37 (Matt 22:41-46; Luke 20:41-44) denies the necessity of a Davidic messiah. In the Q source (Matt 11:2-6; Luke 7:18-23), Jesus bases his messiahship on his miraculous deeds (cf. also Luke 4:16-21).
[2] John 7:40-42.

Nazareth?"[1]  His reaction suggests that Nazareth had a bad reputation and wasn't the kind of place a messiah would come from.

Jesus' followers tried to conceal his birth in Nazareth by saying he was born in Bethlehem. That's why the census taken by Quirinius was backdated to the time of Jesus' birth. It was a literary device to get Mary and Joseph to Bethlehem so Christians could say Jesus was born there.

Walking from Nazareth to Bethlehem on foot took at least five to seven days. Could a woman about to give birth have done that? Could she have walked, or ridden a donkey, hour after hour along a rocky trail in blazing heat? Or slept outside in the cold at night? Or been constantly alert for wild animals and bandits? Could a woman in the last stage of pregnancy have survived a journey like that? Could her unborn child have survived? Considering these and other difficulties, it's highly unlikely that Joseph and Mary ever went to Bethlehem. The odds are against it. So, if Mary and Joseph didn't go to Bethlehem, Jesus wasn't born there. He was born in Nazareth, where his parents lived.

The Gospel of Matthew presents a completely different picture. Joseph and Mary don't go to Bethlehem; they already live there. Wise men "entering the house" refers to the family home.[2]  Herod murders little boys in Bethlehem because he thought that was where his future rival lived. When the family returns from Egypt, they go back to their former home, but don't stay. Bethlehem is still too dangerous for them, so they continue on far north to Nazareth for safety.

The obvious difference between these two accounts proves that both are fictitious.

One more factor is pertinent in this regard. Most people in ancient times were subsistence farmers who tilled small plots of

---

[1] John 1:45-46.
[2] Matt 2:11.

land that demanded constant attention. Then as now, farmers were tied down and couldn't venture far from home. That's difficult to imagine. Today we hop in cars, jump on buses or trains or fly anywhere in the world. Few people today spend their entire lives where they were born—but that's the way it was in ancient times.

Names connected people to where they lived. That's why the gospels refer to "Jesus of Nazareth."[1] Linking him to Nazareth established his identity vis-à-vis men with the same name who lived in other villages. That fact alone identifies Nazareth as Jesus' hometown. It was the village where he was born and raised, the place he "came from."

# Ascension

Acts says that Jesus lived in Jerusalem with his disciples for forty days after rising from the dead.[2] Other sources claim that he stayed on earth for various periods of time ranging from 8 to 550 days.[3] One even stated that he stayed for twelve years before finally rising to heaven!

An interim on earth before rising to heaven served an important purpose. If Jesus had gone directly to heaven, without being seen on earth, no one would have known what happened to his body. It would simply have disappeared, leaving people without a clue as to its whereabouts. without a trace. Stopping on earth before proceeding to heaven let people see Jesus and know he was alive. That's why the fictional post-resurrection stories in the gospels were written. They served as eyewitness accounts of seeing Jesus after he rose from the dead.

---

[1] Mark 1:9, 1:24 (Luke 4:34), 10:47 (Luke 18:37), 16:6. Matt 21:11, 26:71. Luke 29:19. John 1:45, 18:5,7. Acts 2:22, 3:6, 4:10, 6:14, 10:38, 22:8, 26:9.
[2] Acts 1:3.
[3] J. M. Robinson, "Ascension," *The Interpreter's Dictionary of the Bible* (ed. G. A. Buttrick, 4 vols; Nashville: Abingdon, 1962), 1:246.

Two New Testament passages, both written by the same person, purport to describe Jesus' ascension to heaven. The first appears at the end of Luke:

*Then he led them out as far as Bethany, and lifting up his hands, he blessed them. While he was blessing them, he withdrew from them and was carried up into heaven.*[1]

The second is found at the beginning of Acts.

*After his suffering he presented himself alive to them by many convincing proofs, appearing to them during forty days and speaking about the kingdom of God.*[2]

Then, when his time on earth was done,

*. . . as they were watching, he was lifted up and a cloud took him out of their sight. While he was going and they were gazing up toward heaven, suddenly two men in white robes stood by them. They said, "Men of Galilee, why do you stand looking up toward heaven? This Jesus, who has been taken up from you into heaven, will come in the same way as you saw him go into heaven."*[3]

The mythical character of this account, with heaven located high above in the sky, is obvious.

## Mythical Milieu

Ascensions were commonplace in antiquity:

In the Hellenistic world the ascent of a king, prophet, hero, or holy man to the heavens, the place of the gods, was a well-known motif signifying the divine status of the one who ascended. Heracles was deified through an ascension to heaven, and Ganymede became immortal when Zeus lifted him into heaven to serve as cupbearer to the gods. More generally, under the influence of Platonism, all human souls

---

[1] Luke 24:50-51.
[2] Acts 1:3.
[3] Acts 1:9-11.

were believed to be immortal and returned to the heavens when cleansed of their mortal attachments.[1]

Rome's mythical founder Romulus rose to heaven, as did divinized Roman Emperors.[2]

Hebrew scripture says Enoch "walked with God; then he was no more, because God took him."[3] Elijah "ascended in a whirlwind into heaven."[4] Jewish folklore asserts that Levi, Baruch, Ezra, Moses, Zephaniah and Abraham all rose to heaven as well.[5]

In Judaism as in Hellenism:

This tradition merged with that of the soul's ascent in ecstasy or at death, which developed in the Zoroastrian Avesta, Mithraism, Mandaeism, and Gnosticism into a detailed voyage through the three or seven heavenly spheres with their gates, hostile spirits, and other obstacles, to be passed by means of esoteric knowledge, passwords, and the aid of friendly spirits. Syncretistic theology developed the pattern of descent from heaven and ascent to heaven for describing the Gnostic "Redeemer," as well as the "divine men" of the Hellenistic age ... and the Roman Caesar.[6]

The mythical cycle of leaving and returning to heaven appears in the bible. Jacob dreamed of a ladder "set up on earth, the top of it reaching to heaven; and the angels of God were ascending and descending on it."[7] Proverbs asks, "Who has

---

[1] Gregory Shaw, "Ascension of Christ," in *The Oxford Companion to the Bible* (ed. Bruce M. Metzger and Michael D. Coogan; New York: Oxford University Press, 1993), 61.

[2] Suetonius, for example, refers to a high-ranking Roman official who testified that he had seen "the form of the Emperor . . . on its way to heaven." *The Lives of the Caesars; Life of Augustus,* 100:4.

[3] Gen 5:24; Heb 11:5.

[4] 2 Kgs 2:11.

[5] Robinson, IDB 1:245.

[6] Robinson, IDB 1:245.

[7] Gen 28:12.

70

ascended to heaven and come down?"[1]  Escalators, evidently, were imagined long before they appeared in shopping malls!

The same mythical cycle appears in the New Testament. The Gospel of John quotes Jesus as saying, "Very truly, I tell you, you will see heaven opened and the angels of God ascending and descending upon the Son of Man."[2]  Jesus later states, "No one has ascended into heaven except the one who descended from heaven, the Son of Man."[3]  His disciples were shocked when he said they had to eat his flesh and drink his blood, but that was the least of it. "Does this offend you? Then what if you were to see the Son of Man ascending to where he was before?"[4]  He tells Mary Magdalene not to embrace him "because I have not yet ascended to the Father." Then she gives this message to his disciples: "I am ascending to my Father and your Father, to my God and your God."[5]  So, in John, the round trip is clear. The mythical cycle ends in heaven where it began.

## Summary

Christ's preexistence, incarnation, virgin birth and ascension follow the mythological cycle of leaving and returning to heaven. All of these beliefs were part of the mythological landscape of the day.

The line between gods and humans was blurred in antiquity. Gods looked and acted like humans, and humans could turn into gods. Two incidents in the Acts of the Apostles illustrate the difficulty of deciding who was, or was not, a god. The first recounts the healing of a crippled man and its aftermath:

*When the crowds saw what Paul had done, they shouted in the Lycaonian language, "The gods have come down to us in human form!" Barnabas they called Zeus, and Paul they*

---

[1] Prov 30:4a.
[2] John 1:51
[3] John 3:13.
[4] John 6:61-62.
[5] John 20:17.

*called Hermes, because he was the chief speaker. The priest of Zeus, whose temple was just outside the city, brought oxen and garlands to the gate; he and the crowds wanted to offer sacrifice.* [1]

Paul and Barnabas were horrified at the prospect of having a sacrifice offered to them. "Friends," they shouted, "why are you doing this? We are mortals just like you." Yet, "Even with these words, they scarcely restrained the crowds from offering sacrifice to them." Shortly thereafter, however, the crowd had a change of heart:

*But Jews came there from Antioch and Iconium and won over the crowds. Then they stoned Paul and dragged him out of the city.*

After being treated like a god, Paul was beaten and thrown out of town!

The second incident took place while Paul was sailing to Rome under guard to be tried before Caesar. [2] A violent storm arose on the Mediterranean, blowing the ship off course and onto a reef. Fortunately, everyone on board made it to shore through pounding surf. A few of the island's inhabitants eventually appeared and lighted a fire to warm the drenched survivors. As Paul gathered wood for the fire, he was bitten by a poisonous snake.

*When the natives saw the creature hanging from his hand, they said to one another, "This man must be a murderer; although he has escaped from the sea, justice has not al lowed him to live." He, however, shook off the creature into the fire and suffered no harm. They were expecting him to swell up or drop dead, but after they had waited a long time and saw that nothing unusual had happened to him, they changed their minds and began to say that he was a God.* [3]

---

[1] Acts 14:8-19.
[2] Acts 27.
[3] Acts 28:4-6.

72

These two incidents go in opposite directions. In the first, Paul is said to be a god and then stoned, whereas, in the second, he's seen as a murderer before becoming a god! The contrast between these episodes reveals the subjectivity involved in deciding whether someone was a human being or a god. Depending upon the observer's viewpoint, one might easily be the other.

## Conclusion

"Divine men" were familiar figures in antiquity. They included "seers, priests, religious heroes, workers of miracles . . . and especially the great lawgivers of the past." The parallels between those individuals and the mythical figure of Christ are unmistakable.

# PART THREE
# LAST DOGMAS

# Introduction
## Philosophical Christianity

Chapter Five addresses the trinity and Chapter Six deals with the two natures of Christ. The dogma of the trinity declares that God, Christ and the Holy Spirit are one God, not three; and the dogma of Christ's two natures states that, while on earth, Jesus was both human and divine. These dogmas are qualitatively different from those in Parts One and Two. Earlier dogmas were simple and unreflective, whereas these in Part Three are deeply philosophical.

The next two chapters discuss the philosophical ideas that support these dogmas, and the bitter rivalries from which they energed. Like Toto pulling back the curtain hiding the Wizard of Oz, the following chapters discuss the ideas hidden behind these dogmas. These ideas are couched in ancient categories of thought, and are rarely, if ever, encountered today. They may be hard to grasp, but we need to know about them in order to critique the dogmas themselves.

These final dogmas were hammered into shape over centuries, like red-hot steel on an anvil, before being codified in creeds of faith. A detailed account of how that happened lies beyond the scope of this book. An overview is enough to give us a sense of that long and complicated history. A Critical Commentary following these chapters observes that creeds:

- **Tried to settle theological disputes**
- **Were intertwined with politics**
- **Came to exist by chance**
- **Elevated philosophy over faith**
- **Relied upon imaginary concepts**
- **Concealed intellectual arrogance, and**
- **Left a legacy of intolerance**

# Chapter Five
# THE TRINITY

## One God Alone

The first Christians were Jews who believed in one God and one God alone. Morning and evening they prayed the *Shema*:

**"Hear, O Israel:**
**the Lord is our God, the Lord alone."**[1]

This was the bedrock of their faith.

Early Christian writings affirm faith in one God alone. Paul emphatically stated that "no idol in the world really exists," and "there is no God but one."[2] Others said the same:

> According to **Hermas**, the first commandment is to "believe that God is one, Who created and established all things, bringing them into existence out of non-existence." It was He Who "by his invisible and mighty power and great wisdom created the universe, and by His glorious purpose clothed the creation with comeliness, and by His strong word fixed the heavens and founded the earth above the waters."
>
> For **Clement** God is "the Father and creator of the entire cosmos," and for **Barnabas** and the **Didache** "our maker," "the Lord almighty," "the Lord Who governs the whole universe," and "the master of all things."[3]

Belief in one God alone characterized early Christianity, but two other beliefs were just as important.

---

[1] Deut 6:4.
[2] 1 Cor 8:4.
[3] J.N.D. Kelly, *Early Christian Doctrines* (New York: Harper & Brothers, 1958), 83 (my bolding).

# Christ the Lord

Early Christians worshipped the risen Jesus as well as God. As Paul explained, "Even though we once knew Christ from a human point of view, we know him no longer in that way."[1] The New Testament and other early Christian writings leave no doubt about Christ's divinity. As discussed previously, Christians thought of Christ as a divine being who came down from heaven and went back to heaven when his work on earth was done.

Early Christians saw no contradiction in worshipping Christ as well as God. Paul spoke of both in the same breath:

*Indeed, even though there may be so-called gods in heaven or on earth—as in fact there are many gods and many Lords—yet for us there is one God, the Father, from whom are all things and for whom we exist, and one Lord, Jesus Christ, through whom are all things and through whom we exist.*[2]

Paul thought of God as the *source* of all things and Christ as the *means* by which they came into existence.[3] The universe came "from" God "through" Christ. That distinction allowed him to believe in Christ while also believing in only one God. God was "Father," and Christ the "Lord." But that differentiation was problematic. It amounted to **ditheism**, or belief in two Gods. The polytheism of the age undoubtedly kept Paul and other early Christians, as monotheists, from seeing the contradiction involved in worshipping both God *and* Christ.

Pliny, a Roman provincial governor, wrote to Emperor Trajan in 112 CE for advice on how to handle a rogue superstition that was spreading in his province. He had tortured a few members of the sect to find out what they believed, and informed the

---

[1] 2 Cor 5:16.
[2] 1 Cor 8:5-6.
[3] The same thought later appeared in the Gospel of John (1:1-3a) and the Letter to the Hebrews (1:1-3a).

Emperor "that on an appointed day they had been accustomed to meet before daybreak, and to recite a hymn antiphonally to Christ, as to a god."[1] That was typical of Christian worship.

## The Holy Spirit

In addition to worshipping God and Christ, Christians venerated a mysterious "Holy Spirit." As seen in Paul's letters, the Holy Spirit played an essential part in the lives of the earliest Christians.[2] Charismatic phenomena died out at the end of the apostolic age,[3] but the Spirit wasn't forgotten. It lived on in church tradition, enshrined as a hallowed memory in its liturgy, baptismal creeds and confessions of faith.

## God, Christ and the Holy Spirit

An early baptismal creed shows that belief in God, Christ and the Holy Spirit was normative by the second century:

This, then, is the order of the rule of our faith: God the Father, not made, not material, invisible; one God, the creator of all things: this is the **first point** of our faith.

The **second point** is this: the Word of God, Son of God, Christ Jesus our Lord, Who was manifested to the prophets according to the form of their prophesying and according to the Father's dispensation; through Whom (i.e. the Word) all things were made; Who also, at the end of the age, to complete and gather up all things, was made man among men, visible and tangible, in order to abolish death and show forth life and produce perfect reconciliation between God and man

And the **third point** is: the Holy Spirit, through Whom the prophets prophesied, and the fathers learned the things

---

[1] Henry Bettenson, ed., *Documents of the Christian Church* (London: Oxford University Press, 1963), 4.
[2] See, for example, 1 Cor 12-14.
[3] They reappeared at the end of the second century in **Montanism**, and again in modern times in Pentecostalism.

of God, and the righteous were led into the way of righteousness; Who at the end of the age was poured out in a new way upon mankind in all the earth, renewing man to God.[1]

Early Christians had no difficulty worshipping God, Christ and the Holy Spirit. The ancient world was filled with gods and goddesses, so worshipping three Gods was nothing unusual.

But a nagging question remained: how could Christians worship three Gods and still be *monotheists*? Didn't that make them *tritheists*? That was the conundrum Christians faced at the start of the Common Era.

But it wasn't insurmountable. If God, Christ and the Holy Spirit were united as one, all-encompassing deity, Christians wouldn't be tritheists. Technically speaking, they would still be monotheists. That was the dialectic that eventually led to the dogma of the trinity.

However, before that dogma was finalized in the fifth century, Christians engaged in bitter theological disputes that occurred in two overlapping phases. The first addressed Christ's relationship to God in heaven, and the second dealt with the Spirit's relationship to God and Christ.

## The *Logos* and Christ in Heaven

Educated Romans dismissed Christianity as an ignorant superstition.[2] Second century Christian apologists refuted that misconception by representing Christianity as a philosophy. A dominant concept of the day called the ***"Logos"*** helped them in that effort:

---

[1] Kelly, *Doctrines*, 83 (my bolding).
[2] Pliny, for instance, referred to Christianity as "a depraved and extravagant superstition." (Bettenson, *Documents*, 5)

The idea of God's Logos could be found in a variety of sources. It was floating in the air of popular Greek philosophy and Hellenistic Judaism, and had become naturalized in Christian circles by the Prologue of the Fourth Gospel.[1]

In Stoic philosophy, the *Logos* was a universal mind, a "world soul" that pervaded all creation:

The forces in the universe form one all-pervasive force or fire . . . and the ultimate principle is the rational, active soul of the World. Most important of all, the animating principle of things is reason—intelligent, purposeful and good . . . . The rational principle is related to the world as the human soul is related to its body. All life and movement have their source in the logos: it is god; it contains the germs or seeds (spermata) of life; in it the whole cosmos lies potential as the plant in the seed.[2]

The *Logos* was another name for God or, more precisely, an *attribute* of God. The basic meaning of *Logos* in Greek is "word," but it eventually came to mean Reason and Divine Wisdom as well. Encompassing both, the *Logos* was thus an integral part of God's very own being.

The first verse of the Gospel of John echoes the opening verse of Genesis, and identifies the *Logos* as God's agent of creation:

*In the beginning was the Word (**Logos**) and the Word (**Logos**) was with God, and the Word (**Logos**) was God. He was in the beginning with God. All things came into being through him, and without him, not one thing came into being.*[3]

---

[1] Cyril C. Richardson, ed., *Early Christian Fathers* (The Library of Christian Classics, vol. 1; trans Cyril C. Richardson; Philadelphia: The Westminster Press, 1953), 233. The prologue is John 1:1-18.
[2] Frank Thilly, *A History of Philosophy* (rev. Ledger Wood; New York: Holt, Rinehart and Winston, 1962), 134.
[3] John 1:1-3.

The fourth gospel identifies the *Logos*, the Stoic world soul, as Christ! That's astounding, and it led to similar claims.

**Justin Martyr** (100-165 CE) argued that Christ embodied the world soul, the *Logos* itself. The *Logos* was eternal, which meant that people who lived according to the dictates of reason prior to Christ's birth were Christians before Christ.[1] The great philosophers of the past were all likewise inspired by the *Logos* incarnate in Christ:

> . . . the teachings of Plato are (not) different from those of Christ, but they are not in all respects similar, as neither are those of the Stoics and poets and historians. For each man spoke well in proportion to the share he had of the generative word (*spermatikos Logos*). Whatever things were rightly said among all teachers, are the property of us Christians. For next to God, we worship and love the Word (*Logos*).[2]

Identifying Christ as the *Logos* was a step toward explaining how Christ and God were related in heaven. Nevertheless, while seen as the *Logos*, Christ remained subordinate to God.

**Irenaeus** (130-200 CE) linked the *Logos* to the Holy Spirit,[3] saying both existed as thoughts in God's mind prior to creation. Then, emerging from God's mind, they actualized themselves in creating the universe. Once the cosmos was finished, they continued to serve as intermediaries, as God's "hands," in governing the world.

Irenaeus referred to this arrangement as the "economy,"[4] but not in our sense of the word. We think of the "economy"

---

[1] Richardson, *Fathers*, 272.
[2] J. Stevenson, ed., *A New Eusebius: Documents Illustrative of the History of the Church to A.D. 337* (London: S·P·C·K, 1963), 64.
[3] At this early juncture, the Spirit wasn't identified as the third person of the trinity. That wouldn't happen for another two centuries.
[4] *Oikonomia* in Greek means "the management of a household or family" or, more generally, "administration, government of a state." (Liddell and Scott, "*oikovoµía*," 416.)

in financial terms, as Gross Domestic Product (GDP) or international trade. But that's not what Irenaeus meant. In his mind, the "economy" was how the world operated in all its complexity. The idea was similar to the corporate goal of maximizing productivity, and "Home Economics" courses that teach efficient ways of managing a household. The only difference is that Irenaeus had the whole world in mind instead of finances alone.

The concept of the "economy" raised the Spirit's importance. Indeed, without the Spirit:

> . . . it is impossible to behold the Word of God since the knowledge of the Father is the Son, and the knowledge of the Son of God can only be obtained through the Spirit; and . . . the Son ministers and dispenses the Spirit to whomsoever the Father wills, and as He wills.[1]

"Economic trinitarianism" explained how Christ and the Spirit were related to God. It focused on their *functions* instead of their *natures*—what they *did* rather than what they *were*. Nevertheless, inasmuch as both acted as God's "hands," they were inferior to God himself.

## Early Trinitarianism

**Tertullian** (160-220 CE) made Christ and the Spirit equal to God with the help of Stoicism. Stoics thought the universe was composed entirely of matter, ranging from coarse to highly refined. In this schema, "spirit" was the highest and most rarefied form of matter. But that's not how we think of it today. Spirit isn't a "substance"; it's the opposite of matter, devoid of substance.

Physics helps to explain this idea. Hydrogen (H), with an atomic weight of 1.008, is the lightest element in the Periodic Table and the most abundant substance in the universe.

---

[1] Kelly, *Doctrines*, 107.

Invisible with a molecular structure, it aptly illustrates how Stoics conceived of spiritual "substances."

**The dogma of the trinity is based on the concept of "spiritual substances."** Tertullian asserted that God, Christ and the Holy Spirit were one God because all three were made of the same *substantia*:

> All are of one, by unity of substance; while the mystery of the dispensation is still guarded which distributes the unity into a Trinity, placing in their order the three, the Father, the Son, and the Holy Spirit . . . for they are of one substance and one essence and one power, inasmuch as He is one God from whom these degrees and forms and aspects are reckon-ed under the name of the Father, and of the Son, and of the Holy Spirit.[1]

Tertullian, like Irenaeus, maintained that all three worked together in an "economy" governing the world:

> We believe in one only God, yet subject to this dispensation, which is our word for economy, that the one only God has also a Son, His Word, Who issued ut of Himself . . . which Son then sent, according to His promise, the Holy Spirit, the Paraclete, out of the Father.[2]

Tertullian thought that God, Christ and the Holy Spirit shared the same "substance." They formed a *trinitas*[3] of three "persons," but not in our sense of the word. Tertullian's *per-sonas* weren't individual persons; they were the ways in which God acted, whether as himself or Christ or the Holy Spirit. The idea is similar to that of a government acting through its subsi-diary agencies. However, since "Christ" and the "Holy Spirit" were mere labels for ways God acted, they didn't exist in their

---

[1] Williston Walker, *A History of the Christian Church* (rev. ed.; New York: Charles Scribner's Sons, 1959), 66.
[2] Kelly, *Doctrines*, 113.
[3] Tertullian was the first to use the word "trinity" in a technical sense.

own right. They were attributes, or extensions, of God. Understood as such, Tertullian's *personas* fell short of the later orthodoxy that insisted upon each having its own separate identity.

## Monarchianism

The *Logos* theology never appealed to ordinary Christians. As Tertullian observed:

> The simple—I will not call them unwise or unlearned—who always constitute the majority of believers, are startled at the dispensation of the three in one, on the ground that their very rule of faith withdraws them from the world's plurality of gods to the one only true God.[1]

Rank and file Christians saw the "economy" of Father, Son and Spirit as **tritheism**, and insisted that one God alone ruled the universe. Their protest, known as "Monarchianism," took several forms.

**Dynamic Monarchians** held that Jesus received *dunamis,*[2] or power, when he was baptized at the Jordan river.[3] The gift of *dunamis* proved that God adopted Jesus as his very own son. The scripture, "You are my Son, the Beloved; with you I am well pleased," substantiated that belief.

Adoptionists said that, if Jesus were God, *two* Gods would exist:

> If the Father is one and the son another, and if the Father is God and Christ God, then there is not one God, but two Gods are simultaneously brought forward, the Father and the Son.[4]

---

[1] Walker, *History*, 68.
[2] The English word "Dynamite" transliterates *dunamis*.
[3] Mark 1:10-11; Matt 3:16-17; Luke 3:21-22; also, John 1:32.
[4] Kelly, *Doctrines*, 117.

Adoptionism was scriptural, but its idea of Jesus as a man,[1] not God, never garnered popular support.

**Modalistic Monarchians** were different. Like Tertullian, they denied that "Christ" and the "Holy Spirit" existed as independent entities apart from God. They were "modes of operation." That sounds complicated but it's really quite simple. Changing clothes, for example, doesn't change *us*; it only changes what we're *wearing*. The same is true of work. We do different kinds of work but we're the same person no matter what we do. Interpersonal relationships are the best illustrations of Modalism. As Shakespeare observed:

All the world's a stage,
And all the men and women merely players;
They have their exits and their entrances,
And one man in his time plays many parts.[2]

All of us play different roles through life. We act as sons or daughters, husbands or wives, mothers or fathers, grandparents, employees, neighbors, etc. but acting in those capacities doesn't change our underlying identity. We're the same person no matter what role we happen to be playing at any given time. That's Modalism. Playing the part of "Christ" or the "Holy Spirit" didn't change God in any way.

Early Modalism was naïve. If God acted as Christ, then "the Father Himself was born and suffered and died."[3] Modalism also begged the question of who was in charge of the universe while God was on earth acting as "Christ"! Modalism lost its early naivete when **Sabellius** (dates unknown) reframed it in philosophical language in the third century. From then on, Modalistic Monarchianism was called **Sabellianism**.

---

[1] Adoptionism was also called "*Psilanthropism*" (from the Greek *psilos* and *anthropos*, meaning "mere man").

[2] *As You Like It* (Act II, scene VII, line 138).

[3] Walker, *History*, 69. The idea that God, acting as "Christ," suffered and died on the cross is called "*Patripassianism*."

# Eastern and Western Christianity in the Roman Empire

The Roman Empire reached its peak in the early second century CE. It stretched at that point from Germany in the north to northern Africa in the south, and from Egypt and Syria in the east to the British Isles in the west.

Estimates of the Empire's population at that time range from fifty-nine to seventy-six million people spread among a variety of ethnic groups with their own languages and dialects,[1] social customs and religions. This vast array of humanity was held together by Roman military force, a superb network of roads, robust international trade and Roman civil law. Rome itself was situated in the middle of the Empire, with Asia Minor to the east and Europe to the west.

Christianity evolved along different lines in the eastern and western parts of the Empire. Christianity began in the east and spread west from there. This meant that Christians were more numerous in the east than in the west. Apart from that disparity, their mindsets differed. Theologians in the east enjoyed speculative thinking whereas their counterparts in the west were decidedly more pragmatic.

Those mindsets determined their respective approaches to the trinity. Western theologians concentrated on the trinity's *indivisibility*, its "oneness," whereas Eastern theologians focused on its "threeness," the *individuality* of each of its component parts. The uppermost concern in the West was the trinity's *unity*, whereas the East was preoccupied with its *plurality*. The West adopted Tertullian's formula, "One God in three Persons," before the end of the third century, but the East didn't reach an agreement about the trinity until much later.

---

[1] Greek (and later Latin) was the common international language of the time.

As Tertullian's ringing condemnation makes clear, western theologians rejected philosophical interpretations of Christianity.

> Philosophy is the material of the world's wisdom, the rash interpreter of the nature and dispensation of God . . . . What indeed has Athens to do with Jerusalem? What has the Academy to do with the Church? . . . . Away with all attempts to produce a Stoic, Platonic, and dialectic Christianity! We want no curious disputation after possessing Christ Jesus, no inquisition after receiving the gospel! When we believe, we desire no further belief. For this is our first article of faith, that there is nothing which we ought to believe besides.[1]

Tertullian dismissed philosophy but nonetheless found himself relying upon it. Without the Stoic concept of spiritual "substances," the trinity couldn't have been defined as "One God in Three Persons."

Unlike their counterparts in the West, Eastern theologians put philosophy to work in explaining their beliefs. A renowned theological school in Egypt relied upon Platonism and Stoicism. Its first headmaster, **Clement of Alexandria** (150-215 CE), considered philosophy the highest form of rationality, and perfectly suited to convey the truths of Christianity:

> God is the cause of all good things; but of some primarily, as of the Old and New Testament and of others by consequence, as of philosophy. Per chance, too, philosophy was given to the Greeks directly and primarily, till the Lord should call the Greeks. For this was a school-master to bring the Hellenic mind, as the law the Hebrews, to Christ.[2]

Philosophy was superior to faith because it imparted *gnosis*, or knowledge, of Christ.

---

[1] Stevenson, *A New Eusebius*, 178.

[2] Walker, *A History*, 73.

**Origen** (185-254 CE), Clement's successor, was a Platonist who saw the world as the visible expression of an invisible world of ideas that formed patterns for everything in existence.

Platonism is based on the fact that everything starts with an *idea*. Someone in the mist of time conceived of a wheel. Gutenberg pictured a printing press in his mind before constructing one. Paperclips and computer chips were concepts prior to being manufactured. Drawings, diagrams and blueprints are visualized ideas that materialize as products. Without ideas, nothing gets made. Platonism simply extends that fact to the world itself. Everything around us embodies an idea, without which nothing would exist.

Origen thought that human souls originated in that rarefied realm. They were given free will to do as they pleased but misused it to rebel against God. Cast out of that perfect world, they fell to our imperfect world of decay and death. Fortunately, a single soul belonging to Christ stayed true to God and, by entering a human body, reestablished communion between God and the souls that had fallen to earth.

Origen conceived of the universe as a vast hierarchy encompassing space and time. God was at the top of the hierarchy with Christ beneath and the Holy Spirit below Christ.[1] Although lowest in the hierarchy, the Spirit was nonetheless "the most honorable of all the beings brought into existence through the Word, the chief in rank of all the beings originated by the Father through Christ."[2]

Origen was unable to decide how Christ and God were related. He saw their relationship at times as a *moral* union, but at others as a *metaphysical* union. His indecisiveness centered on the question of Christ's *origin*. Was Christ "made," like other creatures on earth, or "begotten" in eternity from God's very own being? Origen's ambiguity on this point led to heated

---

[1] Kelly, *Doctrines*, 128-29.
[2] Kelly, *Doctrines*, 129.

exchanges between those who insisted Christ was "made" on earth, and others who maintained he was "begotten" in eternity. The issue at stake in this disagreement was whether Christ was *subordinate* to God or *equal* to God. That was the sticking point that led to the Arian controversy of the fourth century.

## The Arian Controversy

A conflict ignited by two clerics engulfed churches in the East in the fourth century. It began when **Arius** (250-336 CE), a presbyter, accused **Alexander** (d.328 CE), his Bishop, of preaching Sabellianism ("modes" of God's being). Angered by the criticism, Alexander called a council that declared Arius a heretic. Churches took sides as news of the dispute spread. Many stood with Arius but others backed Alexander.

Arius was a monotheist who boldly stated his beliefs:

We acknowledge one God, Who is alone ingenerate (i.e. self-existent), alone eternal, alone without beginning, alone true, alone possessing immortality, alone wise, alone good, alone sovereign, alone judge of all, etc.[1]

This ringing declaration was based on the idea of spiritual "substances." Arius argued that God's substance couldn't be split because the consequences of splitting it would be disastrous. The splinters of his substance would themselves be Gods, all vying for control of the universe. But that was inconceivable! The proof, therefore, that one God alone ruled the universe was the indivisibility of his substance.

Arianism can be summarized as follows:[2]

- Christ was **created out of nothing** (*ex nihilo).*
- Christ **never existed in eternity.**
  Arians constantly repeated the phrase, "There was when he was not," to make that point.

---

[1] Kelly, *Doctrines,* 227.
[2] Kelly, *Doctrines,* 227-29.

- Christ was **"alien from and utterly dissimilar to the Father's essence and individual being."** In other words, he wasn't God.
- Christ **changed over time and was able to sin.**

## The Council of Nicaea

**Constantine** (272-337 CE) was the first Roman Emperor to look kindly upon Christians. He was said to have seen a cross in the sky with the words, *"En toutō níka"*—"In this (sign) conquer!"—before winning a great battle against Maxentius at the Milvian Bridge outside Rome in 312 CE. He defeated other rivals in the following years, and assumed sole command of the Empire in 323 CE.

Against all odds, the church had grown and become a virtual state within a state by the fourth century. Christians were still a minority, but their internal disputes spilled over into the body politic.

Political instability wasn't tolerated within the Empire, and the conflict roiling churches in the eastern provinces was destabilizing. Something had to be done. Constantine began by urging Arius and Alexander to mend their differences, but they refused. Exasperated by their intransigence, he summoned the churches of the East to Nicaea (in present day western Turkey) to settle the dispute.

He wrote to both men prior to the convocation, telling them that their spat was "of a truly insignificant character and quite unworthy of such fierce contention." He warned them against making the assembly "a mere intellectual exercise," or allowing its proceedings to be "hastily produced in the popular assemblies, nor unadvisedly entrusted to the general ear."[1]

Constantine wanted to end the quarrel as quickly as possible. He had an Empire to govern, and no patience with nit-picking

---

[1] Kenneth Scott Latourette, *A History of Christianity* (New York: Harper and Row, 1953), 153-54.

theologians. Rank and file Christians had no patience with them either. One of them, having survived a recent persecution, expressed disgust with the proposed agenda. Christ, he declared, didn't "teach us dialectics, art, or vain subtleties, but simple-mindedness, which is preserved by faith and good works."[1] Ordinary Christians didn't speak in the debates that followed. The issues were beyond their comprehension.

The council convened in May, 325 CE with more than three hundred bishops in attendance.[2] Some supported Arius, others backed Alexander. Few were trained theologians. Indeed, as one onlooker remarked, most were "simpletons"![3] Constantine ordered the delegates to write—and sign—a statement of faith to end the dispute.[4] All did so except for Arius and two others, who were promptly exiled. With that, on paper at least, the conflict came to an end.

## Aftermath of Nicaea

In reality, however, the creed made the conflict worse by condemning Arians and their beliefs:

But as for those who say, There was when he was not, and, before being born He was not, and that He came into existence out of nothing, or who assert that the Son of God is from a different hypostasis or substance, or is created, or is subject to alteration or change—these the Catholic Church anathematizes.

The creed declared belief:

. . . in one Lord Jesus Christ, the Son of God, begotten from the Father, only-begotten, that is, from the substance (*ousias*) of the Father, God from God, light from light, true God from

---

[1] Latourette, *History*, 154.
[2] This was the First Ecumenical Council, which only six bishops from the West attended.
[3] Walker, *History*, 108.
[4] The full text appears in Appendix A.

true God, begotten not made, of one substance (*homoousion*) with the Father . . . .

Declaring Christ to be "of one substance with the Father" was a direct attack on the Arians' core belief that Christ *wasn't* God.[1] Asserting that he was "God from God, light from light, true God from true God" presumed that "spiritual substances" were real. Being *homoousion*[2] with God meant that Christ was "made" of the same spiritual "stuff" (whatever that might have been!) as God himself. That was a slap in the Arians' faces! But what could they do? Constantine backed the creed, so open opposition was futile. Political intrigue was their only means of resistance.

The Creed was sacrosanct as long as Constantine was alive, but its status changed after he died in 337 CE and left the Empire to **Constantine II** (316-40 CE), **Constans I** (323-50 CE) and **Constantius II** (317-61 CE). The eldest son, Constantine II, died three years later, leaving his inherited share of the Empire to Constans and Constantius.

The two brothers then divided the entire Empire between them, with Constans ruling the West and Constantius the East. Constans supported the creed from Nicaea, but Constantius opposed it. The two maintained an uneasy détente, which came to an end in 350 CE when Constans was murdered by one of his generals. Constantius fought his brother's assassin for three years before finally defeating him in battle. His victory over the usurper put him in sole command of the Empire, at which time he ordered all its churches to adopt Arianism.

---

[1] Arians differed among themselves as to how Christ and God were related. Extremists called "**Anomoeans**" insisted that Christ was completely *unlike* God. Moderates, known as "**Homoeans**," held that Christ was *like* God without defining what "like" meant. Conservatives, dubbed "**Semi-Arians**," said Christ was made of a *similar*, but not the *same*, substance as God. Opposition to the hated term *homoousion* was all that held these diverse groups together.

[2] Pronounced "*homo-OU-sion.*"

Synods implementing Arianism followed.  The first, at Constantius' imperial residence in 357 CE, subordinated Christ to God and forbade the term *"ousia"* (substance).  Those actions effectively negated the creed signed at Nicaea thirty-two years earlier.[1]  A synod held two years later at Nice underscored Christ's subordination to God by saying he was *like* God, but not *equal* to God: "We call the Son *like* the Father, as the holy scriptures call Him and teach."[2]  Later synods at Rimini, Seleucia and Constantinople also affirmed Christ's "likeness" to God.

At that point, it seemed as if Arianism had triumphed.  A church father lamented, "The whole world groaned and marvelled to find itself Arian."[3]  But victory was short-lived.  Constantius fell ill on a military campaign in 361 CE and died at the age of forty-four, leaving his hope for an Empire united by Arianism unfulfilled.

## Last Stages of the Conflict

That Roman Catholicism eventually triumphed over Ariaism was largely due to the efforts of **Athanasius** (296-373 CE), Alexander's successor at Alexandria.  Athanasius held that Christ was generated from God's own substance (*ousia*) like light from the sun or a river from its source.  Christ was part of God, yet existed in his own right:

The Son is of course other than the Father as offspring, but as God He is one and the same; He and the Father are one in the intimate union of Their nature and the identity of Their Godhead . . . thus They are one, and Their Godhead is one, so that whatever is predicated of the Son is predicated of the Father.[4]

Athanasius maintained that Christ and God retained separate identities despite being made of the same substance.

---

[1] Orthodox circles referred to this creed as "The Blasphemy of Sirmium."

[2] Walker, *History*, 113 (my italics).

[3] Kelly, *Doctrines*, 238; citing Jerome (342-420 CE)

[4] Kelly, *Doctrines*, 245.

Athanasius reframed the debate about Christ and God. Instead of dwelling on the issue of "substance," he refocused attention on Christ's role in salvation. The gap existing between God and humans could only be bridged by God. Therefore, by bridging that gap, Christ proved that he was God.

Athanasius saw salvation as a gradual process of divinization: Christ "was made man that we might be made divine."[1] Christ's oneness (*homoousion*) with God was thus the key that united humans with God.

Constantius favored radical Arians over moderates, who were treated like second-class clerics. Athanasius knew of their discontent and, after Constantius' died, invited them to Alexandria, where he proposed an alliance. Nicenes and moderate Arians reconciled their differences at that meeting and closed ranks against Arian radicals.

The conference at Alexandria in 362 CE broke theological ground. Nicenes and moderate Arians agreed that God was one substance (*ousia*) in "three modes of being" (*hypostases*), and also elevated the Holy Spirit to full equality with God and Christ. Those were major steps toward codifying the trinity. However, since the key terms, "substance" and "modes of being" weren't defined,[2] the question of what they were was left unanswered.

## Late Trinitarianism

Including the Holy Spirit in the "substance" (*ousia*) uniting Christ and God was the final step in completing the dogma of the trinity.

As always, the Holy Spirit was a mystery. People hadn't the faintest idea of what it was or did. Irenaeus and Origen had addressed the Spirit but few others even mentioned it. Prior to Nicaea, Christ's relationship to God was the overriding concern.

---

[1] Walker, *History*, 110.
[2] Failing to define crucial terms exacerbated these debates because each side assumed the other knew the meaning of the terms it was using.

That was the issue settled at Nicaea. The creed written there affirmed faith in God and Christ—"and in the Holy Spirit," which was left as an afterthought at the very end. That's all we hear about the Spirit. Nothing else was said. However, after Christ's relationship to God was determined, theologians turned their attention to the Holy Spirit.

Arians had little to say about the Spirit. **Eusebius of Caesarea** (260-340 CE), a moderate Arian known today as the "father of church history," referred to the Spirit as "a third power" that existed "in the third rank."[1]

Nicenes held the Spirit in higher esteem. **Cyril of Jerusalem** (315-86 CE) spoke of it as equal to God and Christ. **Athanasius** went further, saying the Spirit was *homoousion* with both. That was his response to the *Tropici*, a sect that said the Spirit and God were made of different substances. The Tropici thought the Spirit was an angel, and that angels had their own unique substance. Therefore, since the Spirit was an angel, it wasn't part of God's substance.

Athanasius countered that assertion by saying the Spirit and Christ worked together in perfect harmony—harmony which only sharing the same substance made possible. The Spirit was united with God by virtue of sharing the same substance that united Christ and God.[2] Being *homoousion* with God let the Spirit bring humans to God. God, Christ and the Spirit formed an eternal triad indivisibly bound together. This was the view affirmed at Alexandria in 362 CE.

Athanasius died before completing the dogma of the trinity. The task of finishing it was left to the **Great Cappadocians**: Basil the Great (330-79 CE), Gregory of Nazianzus (329-89 CE) and Gregory of Nyssa (330-95 CE).

---

[1] Kelly, *Doctrines*, 255.
[2] This is simple logic: if A equals B and B equals C, then A equals C (If the Spirit equals Christ and Christ equals God, then the Spirit equals God).

The Cappadocians faced the conundrum of incorporating the Holy Spirit into the *homoousion* of Christ and God. People were still mystified by it. Gregory of Nazianzus described the confusion in a Christmas sermon:

> Some consider the Holy Spirit to be a force, others a creature, others God. Others, making the vagueness of scripture their excuse, decline to commit themselves. Of those who acknowledge His deity, some keep it as a pious opinion to themselves, others proclaim it openly, and yet others seem to postulate three Persons possessing deity in different degrees.[1]

The issue at stake in all this was whether the Spirit was, or was not, equal to Christ and God. A sect called the ***Pneumatomachians***, or "Spirit-fighters," rejected the Spirit's equality. They, like the Tropici, insisted that the Spirit was made of a different substance from that uniting Christ and God.

The Cappadocians rejected that idea. Basil defended the Spirit's equality. Gregory of Nyssa declared that God, Christ and the Holy Spirit were made of the same substance because all acted in unison. Gregory of Nazianzus posed, and answered, two rhetorical questions: "Is the Spirit God?" "Yes, indeed!" "Then is he consubstantial?" "Of course, since he is God!"[2] His reasoning was circular, but nonetheless expressed his profound belief in the Spirit's full equality with Christ and God. The Spirit was "not begotten, not created, not fellow-brother nor brother to the Father, not fore-father nor off-spring, but out of the same substance of Father and Son."[3]

But the crux of the difficulty remained: **How could the trinity be *indivisible* without losing the *individuality* of its parts?** The Cappadocians answered that question by saying

---

[1] Kelly, *Doctrines*, 259.
[2] Kelly, *Doctrines*, 261.
[3] Kelly, *Doctrines*, 263.

*all three members of the trinity existed simultaneously within each other.* Basil expressed that idea as follows:

> Everything that the Father is is seen in the Son, and everything that the Son is belongs to the Father. The Son in his entirety abides in the Father, and in return possesses the Father in entirety in Himself.[1]

The reciprocity between Father and Son included the Spirit. The Spirit existed in its entirety within God and Christ, and they in turn existed in their entireties within the Holy Spirit. The co-existence of all three within each other was called *"coinherence,"*[2] meaning that God existed "undivided . . . in divided Persons."[3]

"Coinherence" resolved the final problem in formulating the dogma of the trinity and allayed suspicion that the Cappadocians were Sabellians (Modalists) in disguise. Radical Arians, however, weren't convinced. The idea of God existing "undivided . . . in divided Persons (*hypostases*)" struck them as tritheism. But that missed the point. The Cappadocians insisted that God's *hypostases* (modes of being) were united *within* his substance (*ousia*) and didn't exist apart from it. God's substance was the glue, so to speak, that bound all three together, enabling them to act as one. Conversely, acting in unison proved that all three shared the same substance. So, the charge of tritheism was unwarranted. "In answer to those who upbraid us with tritheism, let it be said that we worship one God, one not in number but in nature."[4]

---

[1] Kelly. *Doctrines*, 264.
[2] It was also known as the *perichoresis*, or "dance," of the divine persons.
[3] Kelly, Doctrines, 264.
[4] Kelly, *Doctrines*, 269.

# The Council of Constantinople

Nicenes grew stronger after Constantius died. Then, in 379 CE, the political winds finally shifted in their favor when **Theodosius I** (347-95 CE) came to the throne. Theodosius despized Arianism as much as Constantius had hated Nicene beliefs. Constantius tried to make Arianism the official faith of the Roman Empire. Now, in a great twist of fate, Theodosius acted to make Roman Catholicism the official faith of the Empire. Arians comprised ninety per cent of all Christians in the East at the time,[1] but were nevertheless compelled to abandon their beliefs. A council held under Theodosius' auspices in 381 CE condemned Arianism and established Roman Catholicism as the official faith of the Roman Empire.[2] Discredited and banned from the Empire, Arianism eventually faded away.[3]

**The Council of Constantinople sealed the victory of Roman Catholicism over Arianism.** After centuries of bitter conflicts, Christians could finally explain how one God was three, and three Gods were one.

---

[1] Adolf Harnack, *Outlines of the History of Dogma* (trans. Edwin Knox Mitchell; Beacon Hill, Boston: Beacon Press, 1959), 265.

[2] This was the Second Ecumenical Council.

[3] Arianism continued for a century or more among Germanic tribes in the north, but gradually died out as they converted to Roman Catholicism.

# SYNOPSIS
## The Trinity

### One God Alone

The first Christians were Jews who believed in one God alone. They also believed in Christ and the Holy Spirit and saw no contradiction in worshipping them as well as God.

### Christ and God

The *Logos* was a philosophical concept, a universal mind, or "world-soul," that pervaded all creation.

The risen Christ was identified as the *Logos*—the "Word" that brought the universe into being—in order to unite him with God.

### Christ and the Holy Spirit

The concept of the "economy," meaning how the world was managed, connected Christ and the Holy Spirit.

### Early Trinitarianism

**Tertullian** united God, Christ and the Holy Spirit in a "trinity" on the basis of all being made of the same "spiritual substance."

Ordinary Christians, however, thought that was *tritheism*, and protested against it by emphasizing the oneness of God. Their protest, called "**Monarchianism**," took two forms: *dynamic* and *modalistic*.

### Eastern and Western Christianity

Christianity evolved along different lines in the eastern and western parts of the Roman Empire. This is apparent in their respective approaches to philosophy in general and the trinity in particular.

### Arianism

Arianism denied that Christ was God.

99

An argument between **Arius** and **Alexander** spread throughout churches in the East.

Emperor **Constantine** called these churches to Nicaea in 325 CE to settle the dispute. However, it continued for years, with Arians gaining the upper hand at one point under **Constantius II**. Constantius wanted to make Arianism the official faith of the Roman Empire but death kept him from doing that.

**Athanasius** is credited with the triumph of Nicene beliefs (Roman Catholicism) over Arianism.

## Late Trinitarianism

Incorporating the Holy Spirit into the *homoousion* ("same substance") of God and Christ was the final step in finishing the dogma of the trinity. The **Great Cappadocians** were instrumental in that effort.

## The Council of Constantinople (381 CE)

**Theodosius I** (d.395) despised Arianism as much as Constantius, years earlier, had hated Nicene beliefs. A council held under his auspices in the Capitol outlawed Arianism and made Roman Catholicism the official faith of the Empire.

# Chapter Six
## THE TWO NATURES
## OF CHRIST

The dogma of the trinity explains how Christ, God and the Holy Spirit were related *in heaven*, whereas the dogma of Christ's two natures deals with how Jesus could have been both human and divine while *on earth*.

As discussed in Chapter Three, early Christians thought of Christ as a divine being who left heaven to come to earth. That's why they spoke of an "incarnation." It marked the moment he transitioned from eternity and entered the world of space and time. But that presented a problem. How could a *divine* being become a *human* being? "Spirit" and "flesh" are opposites. Paul spoke of their incompatibility in Galatians: "For what the flesh desires is opposed to the Spirit, and what the Spirit desires is opposed to the flesh."[1] Like oil and water, the two don't mix. They're mutually exclusive. So, how could both coexist in the same person? How could the earthly Jesus have been divine as well as human? The dogma of Christ's dual natures attempts to reconcile what were, in effect, his "dueling" natures.

### One-sided Solutions

The problem of Christ's dual natures was avoided altogether by saying he was one or the other, but not both—either human but not divine, or divine not human. Jewish Christians known as **Ebionites** said that, apart from being empowered by the Holy Spirit, Christ was no different from any other man. Mary his mother was an ordinary mortal as well:

> Mary did not bear the Word, for Mary did not exist before the ages. Mary is not older than the Word; what she bore

---

[1] Gal 5:17.

was a man equal to us, but superior in all things as a result of holy spirit.[1]

**Docetists** claimed that Jesus was a phantom who only *looked* like a man.[2] The idea that Jesus wasn't a real human being was widespread in early Christianity. In the words of an early father of the church, "There are some who declare that Jesus Christ did not come in the flesh but only as a spirit, and exhibited an appearance of flesh."[3] Docetism threatened belief in Jesus' humanity well into the second century.

**Gnosticism** posed a similar threat. Gnostics asserted that Jesus' body was made of a psychic substance, not flesh and blood. They delighted in devising abstruse metaphysical systems too complicated to be understood,[4] and derided ordinary Christians as simpletons. They dismissed beliefs like Jesus' physical resurrection as crude and recast them in spiritual terms. As seen in the writings of many early church fathers, Gnosticism posed a serious threat to the church's belief in Jesus as a flesh-and-blood human being.

**Marcion** (d.190 CE), an influential lay person in the church at Rome, was another who denied that Jesus had been a mortal man. In his opinion, the being called "Jesus" was none other than God himself walking on earth.

## The *Logos* and Christ on Earth

The *Logos* explained Christ's divine nature on earth as well as his relationship to God in heaven. Explaining how it interacted with his human nature, however, was challenging. Did the *Logos* live *inside* Jesus' body or *become* his body? Did it snatch Jesus' body like an alien from outer space? Or fill it like water inside a bottle, or a hermit crab within a shell? Was Jesus a mere puppet, and the *Logos* a divine puppeteer? How could a

---

[1] Kelly, *Early Christian Doctrines*, 140.
[2] "Docetism" comes from the Greek verb *dokein*, meaning "to seem."
[3] Kelly, *Early Christian Doctrines*, 141. (cf. 1 John 4:1-3; also 2 John 7).
[4] "Gnosticism" comes from the Greek noun *gnōsis,* meaning "knowledge."

mortal body interact with an immortal *Logos*? Did they cooperate? Were they equal? Or did one dominate the other? Those were the questions to be answered.

## Christ's Two Natures in the West

Tertullian was the first to see the problem with Christ's having two incompatible natures. He wasn't satisfied with saying the *Logos* became incarnate; he wanted to know *how* that happened. How could an immortal Spirit become mortal flesh?

> But this provokes the inquiry how the Word became flesh. Was he, so to speak, metamorphosed into flesh, or did he clothe himself in it?[1]

Did the *Logos transform* Christ's flesh, or *wear* it like a garment? That was the question. Tertullian dismissed transformation because it dissolved both in a *tertium quid* unlike either. Christ's flesh disappeared, and the purity of the *Logos* was lost by being mixed with human flesh.

Being "clothed" in Christ's flesh was a better option because it kept both apart, thus preserving their essential natures. Christ's flesh wouldn't disappear if worn like a garment, and the *Logos* wouldn't lose its purity by being mixed with it. Separating both also meant that Christ's human weaknesses could be ascribed to his flesh, and his miracles to the *Logos*. While independent, both natures worked together in perfect harmony: "We observe a twofold condition, not confused but conjoined, Jesus, in one Person at once God and man."[2]

## Christ's Two Natures in the East

Eastern theologians argued over how Christ's human and divine natures interacted. A renowned theological school in Egypt focused on Christ's *divine* nature, while another in Syria emphasized his *human* nature.

---

[1] Kelly, *Early Christian Doctrines*, 151.
[2] Kelly, *Early Christian Doctrines*, 151.

# The School of Alexandria

Alexandrian theologians were inspired by the Greek ideal of *apatheia*, or freedom from passion. In their minds, Christ had no human weaknesses. His "inner man," the *Logos*, kept him from suffering and made his mind a mirror image of itself, unencumbered by human thoughts.

**Origen** taught at this school. In words as crude as any spoken by Modalistic Monarchians, he declared:

> . . . the very Logos of the Father, the Wisdom of God Himself, was enclosed within the limits of that man who appeared in Judaea; nay more, that God's Wisdom entered a woman's womb, was born as an infant, and wailed like crying children.[1]

Origen said that the *Logos* governed Christ's thoughts and actions, making him, in effect, an automaton, a body without a mind, incapable of acting independently or saving anyone. The *Logos* alone did the work of salvation.

Alexandrian theologians acknowledged a human mind in Christ, but it was merely theoretical. The *Logos* controlled him. It vivified his flesh and directed his thoughts, thereby guaranteeing the perfect completion of God's will on earth without interference from a human will.

Identifying Christ as the *Logos* was both a strength and weakness of Alexandrian theology. It invariably raised the question of whether the *Logos* died when Christ died on the cross. **Athanasius** answered that question by positing the *Logos'* existence in *two* different forms: one eternal and the other temporal. That allowed him to assert that the *temporal Logos* died on the cross while the *eternal Logos* escaped unscathed. Positing the *Logos'* existence in different forms also allowed him to assign Christ's human weaknesses to the temporal *Logos*, and his miracles to the eternal *Logos*.

---

[1] Kelly, *Early Christian Doctrines*, 154.

**Apollinarius** (310-90 CE) was the most radical representative of this school. Like other Alexandrians, he denied the possibility of a perfect divine nature and an imperfect human nature coexisting. Two governing principles working at cross purposes would make unified or consistent action impossible. That's why they couldn't coexist. Apollinarius solved that problem by eliminating Christ's human nature and making him totally divine. One completely divine nature preserved Christ's psychic unity and avoided any potential conflict with the *Logos*:

> The flesh is not of itself a complete living entity, but in order to become one enters into fusion with something else. So it united itself with the heavenly governing principle (i.e. the Logos) and was fused with it . . . . Thus out of the moved and the mover was compounded a single living entity—not two, nor one composed of two complete, self-moving principles.[1]

Absolved of humanity, Christ embodied the *Logos*. It became the Alpha and Omega of his existence, directing all his thoughts and actions. The belief that Christ was completely divine without a trace of humanity is known as **Apollinarianism.**

## The School of Antioch

Antiochian theologians rejected all these ideas. Christ's body wasn't a mere container for the *Logos*, or an inert mass of divinized protoplasm. On the contrary, it was just like ours. Alexandrian theologians were Platonists who separated body and soul. Antiochian theologians were Aristotelians who combined both in a holistic union. They upheld Jesus' humanity and, in doing so, became the first to see him as an historical figure.

**Theodore of Mopsuestia** (c.350-428 CE) was the foremost theologian of this school. He championed Christ's full

---

[1] Kelly, *Early Christian Doctrines*, 291-92.

humanity and cited scripture to show he was tempted, got hungry and thirsty, wept, suffered and died like any other human being.

Theodore was emphatic about Christ's humanity: "He took not only a body but a complete man, composed of a body and an immortal soul."[1]

Theodore distinguished between the *Logos* and Christ's human nature, but insisted they acted as one. Alexandrians, however, accused him of preaching "two Sons"—Christ *and* the *Logos*. But that missed the point. While distinct, both worked together in perfect harmony:

> Thus there results neither any confusion of the natures nor any untenable division of the Person; for our account of the natures must remain unconfused, and the Person must be recognized as indivisible.[2]

## Conflict between Alexandrians and Antiochians

The acrimony between these two schools burst into the open when **Nestorius** (d.451 CE) became Patriarch of Constantinople in 428 CE. Nestorius studied at Antioch and, like Theodore, advocated the full humanity of Christ. The dispute began when Nestorius issued an edict forbidding the use of *"Theotokos,"* meaning "Mother of God" or "God-bearing," as a title for Mary. Alexandrians venerated the Virgin, and *Theotokos* expressed their belief that Mary gave birth to God, not a man.

Antiochians spoke of Mary as *"Christotokos,"* or "Christ-bearing," because they believed she gave birth to a man, not God. The idea of a woman bearing God was preposterous, and speaking of God as suffering, dying on the cross and rising from the dead even more absurd. But that's how Alexandrians spoke. They saw about Christ and God as one and the same.[3]

---

[1] Kelly, *Early Christian Doctrines*, 304.

[2] Kelly, *Early Christian Doctrines*, 307.

[3] Speaking of God and Christ as if no different was called the *communicatio idiomatum*, meaning "reciprocity of attributes."

Antiochians, on the other hand, distinguished between them. Christ wasn't God and God wasn't Christ. Anthropomorphisms that referred to God in human terms were anathema to them.

Nestorius differentiated between Christ's human and divine natures in order to safeguard their separate identities. Maintaining that distinction kept Christ's flesh from being absorbed by the *Logos*, and it protected the *Logos* against contamination by his human flesh. Nevertheless, although distinct, both natures worked together like conjoined twins:

> God the Word, and the man in whom He came to be are not numerically two; for the Person of both was one in dignity and honour, worshipped by all creation, in no way and at no time divided by difference of purpose or will.[1]

Nestorius was unequivocal about the bond uniting God and Christ:

> Christ is indivisible in His being Christ, but He is two-fold in His being God and man . . . . We know not two Christs or two Sons or Only-begottens or Lords, not one and another Son, not a first and a second Christ, but one and the same, Who is seen in His created and His increate natures.[2]

**Cyril** (d.444 CE), the reigning Patriarch of Alexandria, was outraged by the edict against *Theotokos*. He and Nestorius were bitter rivals, and Cyril struck back by accusing Nestorius of dividing Christ. The charge, as just seen, was false but it stuck. Separating Christ's two natures was later known as **Nestorianism**.

---

[1] Kelly, *Early Christian Doctrines*, 313-14.
[2] Kelly, *Early Christian Doctrines*, 314.

Cyril said the *Logos* replaced a human mind in Christ,[1] but Nestorius maintained that Christ had a fully functioning human mind that was independent of the *Logos*.[2]

Cyril asserted that Christ's flesh was deified and that, without its having been deified, Christ would have been no different from any other man. Moreover, without his having had deified flesh, the Eucharist would devolve into a cannibalistic rite. Cyril thought Christ was the *Logos* made visible. Understood as such, his defense of *Theotokos*, Mary the "Mother of God," makes perfect sense.

## Attack and Counterattack

Cyril and Nestorius engaged in a heated exchange of letters that went nowhere. The impasse was broken when Cyril appealed to **Pope Celestine I** (d.432 CE) for help. A papal council summoned without Nestorius ordered him to retract his edict against *Theotokos* or be excommunicated. Cyril was charged with delivering the order to him in person in Constantinople. However, before arriving—and without the council's knowledge—he attached twelve "anathemas" of his own that targeted specific points in Nestorius' teaching. Antiochians were enraged by Cyril's anathemas, and dismissed them as blatantly Apollinarian (one completely divine nature).

Cyril's thirst for revenge wasn't slaked by getting the judgement against Nestorius. He went on to petition Emperor **Theodosius II** (401-50 CE) for his removal from the Patriarchate of Constantinople. A council was called for Ephesus in June 431 CE[3] to determine Nestorius' fate but, yet again, Cyril proved treacherous. He and his fellow Alexandrians arrived before

---

[1] Cyril referred to the relationship between Christ and the *Logos* as a "*hypostatic union*" in which Christ's flesh existed in theory but was otherwise indistinguishable from the *Logos*.

[2] Nestorius spoke of the relationship between Christ and the *Logos* as a "*conjunction of natures*," but Alexandrians saw that as a moral link inferior to the indissoluble metaphysical bond they advocated.

[3] The Third Ecumenical Council.

anyone else and excommunicated Nestorius! The Antiochians arrived four days later and, hearing of this, excommunicated Cyril in return! After arriving several weeks late, the Pope's delegates surveyed the impasse and ruled in Cyril's favor. Nestorius fled back to Antioch, where he eventually ended his days in obscurity in a desert monastery.

## Attempted Reconciliation

**Pope Xystus III** (d.440 CE) attempted to conciliate both parties by bringing them together. Negotiations ensued that produced the "Symbol of Union," a compromise hardliners on both sides vilified. Nevertheless, despite widespread dissatisfaction, both parties accepted the Symbol and agreed to a truce.

## Reignited Conflict

The truce came to an abrupt end when **Dioscorus** (d.454 CE) replaced Cyril as Patriarch of Alexandria. Dioscorus was as unscrupulous a cleric as his predecessor, and reignited the smoldering feud by declaring the Alexandrian "one nature" doctrine superior to the "two natures" doctrine advocated at Antioch.

The situation was aggravated by **Eutyches** (378-454 CE), abbot of a large monastery outside Constantinople, who argued that Christ had "two natures *before* the Incarnation, but only one nature *after* the Incarnation."[1] In other words, that Christ was divine *and* human while in heaven, but divine only while on earth! Eutyches supported the Alexandrian "one nature" doctrine but didn't comprehend it. The Antiochian Patriarch of Constantinople was displeased by having Alexandrian ideas propagated in the Capitol and called a council that excommunicated the abbot. Eutyches appealed to **Pope Leo I** (d. 461 CE) in Rome for clemency but the Pope dismissed his appeal. Nevertheless, Eutyches was undeterred. He had powerful friends at

---

[1] F. L. Cross, ed., *The Oxford Dictionary of the Christian Church.* (London, Oxford University Press, 1958), 278.

the imperial court who intervened with the Emperor on his behalf.

A council was called for Ephesus in 449 CE to review Eutyches' excommunication, but Dioscorus dominated it from start to finish. The Pope's delegates weren't allowed to speak, and Eutyches' excommunication was annulled. The hated symbol of Union was anathematized along with the "two natures" doctrine, and Antiochian bishops were driven from their churches. When Pope Leo learned of these high-handed actions, he denounced the council as a "band of robbers" (*latrocinium*). The label stuck, and the council went down in church history as the "Robber Synod of Ephesus."

## The Council of Chalcedon

Theodosius backed the Robber Synod, but his support ended when he fell off his horse and died in 450 CE. **Marcian** (396-457 CE), a professional soldier and staunch Antiochian, took the throne and acted to reverse the decrees of the Robber Synod. A council held the following year at Chalcedon,[1] across the Bosporos Strait from Constantinople, attracted more than five hundred bishops. The assembled prelates annulled the decrees of the Robber Synod, reinstated Eutyches' excommunication, and reaffirmed the creeds written at Nicaea in 325 and Constantinople in 385.

**Eutychianism** (one wholly divine nature) and **Nestorianism** (two separate natures) were anathematized as Christological heresies.

The council tried to balance Christ's human and divine natures by affirming the beliefs of both schools:[2]

We, then, following the holy Fathers, all with one consent, teach men to confess one and the same Son, our Lord Jesus

---

[1] The Fourth Ecumenical Council. Only four bishops came from the West.
[2] The full text appears in Appendix B.

Christ, the same perfect in Godhead and also perfect in man hood; truly God and truly man . . . .

Christ's two natures were defined as coexisting in:

. . . one and the same Christ, Son, Lord, Only-begotten, in two natures, inconfusedly, unchangeably, indivisibly, inseparably, the distinction of natures by no means taken away by the union, but rather the property of each nature being preserved, and concurring in one person and one subsistence (*hypostasis*), not parted or divided into two persons.

Antiochians were heartened by hearing Christ was "in all things like unto us," and agreed with his two natures existing "inconfusedly, unchangeably, indivisibly, inseparably, the distinction of natures by no means taken away by the union."

Alexandrians, for their part, were placated by the definition of Christ's two natures "concurring in one person and one subsistence, not parted or divided into two persons." Bestowing the title *Theotokos,* "Mother of God," upon Mary, and identifying Christ with the *Logos* also appealed to them.

Moderates on both sides accepted the compromise, but extremists in both camps rejected it.

## Nestorians

Left-wing Antiochians objected to the definition of Christ's two natures as "concurring in one person and one subsistence, not parted or divided into two persons." The title *"Theotokos"* given to Mary was another reason for rejecting the creed. They fled to Persia, where opposition to the Roman church stood them in good favor. Nestorius died in obscurity, but his teachings flourished in Persia, spread to India and eventually reached China.

## Monophysites

Right-wing Alexandrians rejected the creed for saying Christ was "truly man, in all things like unto us," and founded Monophysite (one nature) churches in Egypt, Syria and Armenia that continued worshipping Christ as completely divine.

Roman Catholics tried to bring Monophysites back into the fold, but failed. The final stumbling block was whether Christ had *one* divine will, or *two* wills—divine *and* human. A council in Constantinople[1] ultimately ruled that Christ had:

> two natural wills or willings not contrary one to the other . . . but His human will follows, not as resisting or reluctant, but rather as subject to His divine and omnipotent will.[2]

With that, the matter was settled for Roman Catholics.

Islam's rise to power ended all these discussions. The conquests of Damascus (635 CE), Jerusalem and Antioch (638 CE), and Alexandria (641 CE) split the old Roman Empire asunder. From then on, Monophysites in the East and Roman Catholics in the West went their separate ways.

# Conclusion

After centuries of internal strife, the oil and water of Christ's human and divine natures were finally mixed. The alchemy of metaphysics had worked its wonders.

---

[1] The Sixth Ecumenical Council (680-81 CE).
[2] Walker, *History*, 147.

# SYNOPSIS
## The Two Natures of Christ

### Early One-sided Solutions

Jesus was a *man*:

**Ebionites**: Jesus was a human being like everyone else.

Jesus was *not* a man:

**Docetists**: Jesus was a phantom who *looked* like a man.

**Gnostics**: Jesus' body was a psychic substance, not flesh and blood.

**Marcion**: Jesus was God himself walking on earth.

### Western Christianity

**Tertullian**: "One God in Three Persons."

### Eastern Christianity

The **School of *Alexandria*** focused on Christ's *divinity.*

**Origen** equated Jesus with the *Logos.*

**Apollinarius** said Jesus was totally divine with no trace of humanity.

The **School of *Antioch*** emphasized Christ's *humanity.*

**Theodore of Mopsuestia** championed the full humanity of Christ.

### Conflict between Alexandrians and Antiochians

**Nestorius**, Patriarch of *Constantinople*, issued an edict banning the title, "Mother of God" *(Theotokos),* for Mary.

**Cyril**, Patriarch of *Alexandria*, was outraged by the edict, obtained a papal judgement against Nestorius and petitioned Emperor Theodosius II to remove him as Patriarch of Constantinople.

Nestorius was deposed and excommunicated.

Alexandrians and Antiochians agreed to a truce called the **Symbol of Union.**

**Dioscorus** (d.454 CE), Cyril's successor at Alexandria, ended the truce by declaring the Alexandrian "one nature" doctrine superior to the "two natures" doctrine held at Antioch.

**Eutyches** (d.454 CE), abbot of a monastery outside Constantinople, inflamed the situation by advocating a muddled version of the Alexandrian "one nature" doctrine.

The **"Robber Synod of Ephesus"** condemned Antiochians, But Theodosius II's death ended his support for the synod.

**Marcian** (d.457), a staunch Antiochian, replaced him on the throne and acted to reverse the decrees of the Robber Synod.

## The Council of Chalcedon (451 CE)

The Christological extremes of **Eutychianism** (one divine nature) and **Nestorianism** (separate human and divine natures) were condemned as heresies.

Christ's human and divine natures were affirmed.

Extremists in both camps refused to compromise. **Nestorians** fled to Persia, and **Monophysites** started their own churches.

# Critical Commentary

Centuries of unquestioned acceptance have surrounded the dogmas of the trinity and Christ's two natures with a mystique that discourages criticism. Nevertheless, despite their aura of sanctity, these dogmas didn't drop from heaven. As seen over the course of the last two chapters, they were hammered out on the anvil of conflict between men bitterly opposed to one another.

**Dogmas are codified in creeds of faith.**

Therefore, in order to critique these final dogmas, we need to look at the creeds that enshrine them. The following seven critiques target the creeds from Nicaea and Chalcedon but are generally applicable to other creeds as well.

## 1. Creeds tried to settle theological disputes

The creeds that codify these dogmas weren't composed in calm academic environments. They were forged amid fierce debates, personal rivalries and political conflicts. The creed from Nicaea attacked Arianism, and the creed written at Chalcedon attempted to settle a bitter dispute between theological schools at Alexandria and Antioch.

These ancient disputes were vicious. One's eternal destiny, heaven or hell, hung in the balance. The issues at stake seem trivial today, but they were matters of ultimate concern at the time. All had a bearing on eternity. That's why they were so important—and why losers were excommunicated.

Ecclesiastical disputes often sprang from jealousy. The patriarchs of five great cities—Rome, Constantinople, Alexandria, Jerusalem and Antioch—vied with one another for power and influence.[1] As the Empire's Capitol and site where Peter and Paul were martyred, Rome claimed preeminence. Constantinople claimed that same preeminence when it replaced Rome as

---

[1] Justinian I (527-565 CE) called these cities the "Pentarchy."

Capitol of the Empire.[1]  Alexandria was a great city, the second largest in the Empire after Rome, a bustling port and cosmopolitan center of learning on the Eastern Mediterranean.  Jerusalem was where Christ rose from the dead and the church itself began.  Jesus' followers were first called "Christians" at Antioch,[2] the third largest city in the Empire and a vital center of Christianity in Syria.  The patriarchs of these five cities considered themselves most important and viewed each other with suspicion, more as rivals than brothers.

The rivalries got vicious.  Patriarchs nursed grudges and planned vendettas.  Alexander hated Arius, and Cyril ruined Nestorius.  Animosities like those were common at the time.  Talking the talk, then as now, was easier than walking the walk.

## 2.  Creeds were intertwined with politics

Religion and politics have been opposite sides of the same coin throughout history.  Egyptian pharaohs and Roman Caesars were treated like gods.  Kings ruled by "divine right" in the middle ages.  Popes amassed fortunes, owned vast estates and raised armies.  The historical conflict between Catholics and Protestants in northern Ireland is proof of the difficulty of disentangling religion and politics.  The adulation of Donald Trump by evangelical Christians in the United States is further evidence of the intermingling of politics and faith.[3]  Like Esau,[4] Evangelicals have traded their birthright for a taste of MAGA stew.  Psychologically, if not legally, religion and politics are still bound together.

In the Roman Empire, as elsewhere in the ancient world, politics and religion went hand-in-hand.  Constantine summoned churches to Nicaea in 325 CE to end the Arian controversy.  If

---

[1] Constantinople became the new Capitol of the Empire in 324 CE.
[2] Acts 11:26.
[3] This was the case in Germany when Hitler was hailed as a new messiah. *The Theological Declaration of Barmen* (1934) spoke out against Nazi control of the church.
[4] Gen 25:29-34.

that council hadn't been held, the Nicene Creed wouldn't have been written. Marcian convened a council at Chalcedon in 451 CE to reverse the decrees of the Robber Synod. If that council hadn't met, the creed that defines Christ's human and divine natures wouldn't exist. Constantius II tried to impose Arianism on all the churches of the Empire, but death kept him from doing so. Twenty years later, a council called by Theodosius I outlawed Arianism and made Roman Catholicism the official faith of the Empire. Theodosius II supported Cyril against Nestorius and backed the Robber Synod of Ephesus.

Roman Emperors increasingly intruded upon church affairs as the Empire declined. Funds from the imperial treasury were used to subsidize churches and pay clergy salaries. The power of the purse let emperors control the church, which was seen as their last hope for retaining the glory that was Rome.

So, theological debates didn't take place in a vacuum. They had a profound impact on the political stability of the Empire itself.

## 3. Creeds came to exist by chance

If Constantius II hadn't died from an illness, Arianism might have become the official faith of the Roman Empire. Similarly, if Theodosius II hadn't succumbed after falling off his horse, Marcian wouldn't have come to the throne and the Council of Chalcedon wouldn't have taken place.

Pious believers might say those deaths were providential, and that Christianity as known today wouldn't exist if Constantius and Theodosius hadn't died before their time. That, however, would be "special pleading"—assuming one's own beliefs are true, and the beliefs held by others are false.

It also presumes that God caused their deaths. But is that true? Did God make Constantius sick, or throw Theodosius off his horse?

First-century Jews commonly thought of God as a distant Deity with little interest in their everyday lives. But not Jesus.

God was as close to him as an "abba."[1] "Abba," literally translated from Aramaic, means "daddy." It's what little children called their fathers, and that's how Jesus talked to God.

Which leads to the question: How could a good God—a God Jesus trusted as his "Abba"—do such things?

Jesus repudiated the idea that God loves some people but not others. That was the point in his parable about a good Samaritan.[2] Our "neighbor" is anyone who needs our help, regardless of what we might think about that person. The Sermon on the Mount makes the same point. It rejects the notion that God prefers certain people over others:

*Love your enemies . . . so that you may be children of your Father in heaven;* **for he makes his sun rise on the evil and on the good, and sends rain on the righteous and on the unrighteous.**[3]

So, God has no favorites. He accepts everyone,[4] even when we don't.[5]

Christianity might be entirely different today if those two emperors hadn't died early deaths. Orthodox beliefs would be heretical, and heretical beliefs orthodox! If Constantius had recovered from his illness, Jesus wouldn't be God; and if Theodosius had survived his fall, Jesus wouldn't be seen as having been human.

These last dogmas represent the triumphs of one group of ancient Christians over another. That "Victors write history!" is true of all those early theological battles. Winners determined the future course of Christianity, and losers were left behind.

---

[1] Mark 14:36; also Rom 8:15, Gal 4:6.
[2] Luke 10:29-37.
[3] Matt 5:44-45 (my italics).
[4] Matt 20:1-16.
[5] Luke 6:35-36.

## 4. Creeds elevated philosophy over faith

Christianity is based on the belief that Christ rose from the dead. As Paul said, "If you confess with your lips that Jesus is Lord and believe in your heart that God raised him from the dead, you will be saved."[1] No one needed to believe anything else to be a Christian.

However, as time went on, *ideas* about Jesus superseded *faith* in Jesus. The gospel was a philosophy by the end of the second century, and explicated in metaphysical terms by the fourth. Philosophy permeated the intellectual atmosphere of the time, and theologians made use of Stoic, Neo-Platonic and Aristotelian ideas I to convey the gospel. Even philosophy's opponents relied upon it. Tertullian declared, "What has Athens to do with Jerusalem?" but, without the Stoic concept of "spiritual substances," he couldn't have defined the trinity as "One God in three Persons."

Creeds of faith illustrate the transition from faith to philosophy. The terms employed—*homoousios, hypostasis*, etc.—provided philosophical rationales for inherently illogical ideas.

Adolf Harnack, a nineteenth century German theologian, argued that ecclesiastical dogmas expressed "intellectual Christianity," a Christianity of the mind rather than the heart:

Therefore there is always the danger that as knowledge it may supplant faith, or connect it with a doctrine of religion, instead of with God and a living experience.[2]

**Faith as intellectual assent to *propositions* about God, instead of *trust* in God, destroys the very fabric of the gospel.**

---

[1] Rom 10:9.

[2] Harnack, *Outlines*, iv.

The apostles were illiterate.[1]  Early Christians came from the lowest classes of Roman society,[2] and many were slaves.[3] Tertullian spoke condescendingly of "simple believers" who couldn't grasp the concept of three Gods in one.  Constantine told Alexander and Arius not to make Nicaea an "intellectual exercise," or let its proceedings be publicized.

As a religious philosophy, Christianity appealed to intellectuals.  It became the province of theologians, a fascinating game which only they could play.  However, in playing it, they ripped the gospel from the soil that anchored it.

# 5.  Creeds relied upon imaginary concepts

Metaphysics is a branch of philosophy that deals with matters beyond the physical world.  It's defined as *"a priori* speculation upon questions that are unanswerable to scientific observation, analysis or experiment."[4]  The operative term in that definition is *"a priori* speculation*"* or, as might be said, *imagination.*  Metaphysics builds castles in the air and weaves theories out of whole cloth—which means that dogmas couched in metaphysical language are nothing more than smoke and mirrors.

## God's "substance"

The ancient concept of "spiritual substances" illustrates the vacuous nature of metaphysical dogmas.  As discussed in Chapter Five, the concept of spiritual substances arose in Stoicism, which maintained that everything in the universe, visible or invisible, was made of matter.  In Stoicism, "spirit" wasn't an

---

[1] Acts 4:13. The word used to describe them is *agrammatoi*, which means "unable to write, illiterate."  The passage also speaks of them as *idiōtai,* which in this context means "laymen" without any religious training.  The term eventually acquired the derogatory sense of "idiot."
[2] 1 Cor 1:26-29.
[3] Titus 2:9-10.  See also the Letter to Philemon.
[4] "Metaphysics", *The American Heritage Dictionary of the English Language*, fourth edition (Boston: Houghton Mifflin Company, 2000), 1104.

abstraction; it was a rarefied form of matter, a physical substance like hydrogen that couldn't be seen.

**The dogma of the trinity rests upon the idea of "spiritual substances."**

It declares that God, Christ and the Holy Spirit are "made" of the same "substance" and, therefore, *homoousion* with each other. But is that true? Do spiritual "substances" really exist—or are they figments of ancient imagination? We conceive of "spirit" as the *antithesis* of matter—immaterial, ineffable, ethereal—operating unseen like "dark energy" within the fabric of the universe. The notion of "spiritual substances" is at odds with modern thinking.

Therefore, **if "spiritual substances" don't exist, the trinity itself doesn't exist.**

Picture the capstone of an arch. If it's removed, the arch collapses. The same is true of the trinity. If "spiritual substances" aren't real, the *homoousion* of God, Christ and the Holy Spirit doesn't exist. It's a figment of metaphysical imagination. That's critical to realize. Remove the *homoousion* that binds all three together, and the dogma of the trinity collapses like an arch without a capstone.

In all honesty, the dogma of the trinity doesn't make sense. One God can't be three, and three Gods can't be one. It defies logic. Tertullian should have listened to the "simple believers" who couldn't grasp the concept of three Gods in one and rightly called it out as tritheism.

**The dogma of the trinity amounts to metaphysical legerdemain.** Circles can't be squared and the mathematical laws of the universe are immutable. $1+1=2$. It always has, and always will. Nothing, not even God, can change that simple equation.

## 6. Creeds concealed intellectual arrogance

What could be more audacious than trying to analyze God? Yet that's precisely what ancient theologians were doing. They delved into ontology—"being" itself—and attempted to dissect God as if he were a lab specimen. To be fair, the men who did this were trying to comprehend the faith they professed.[1] However, in doing so, they concocted artificial mental constructs devoid of substance. It was a great game and challenged intellects at a time when little else did. But it was vacuous, an empty exercise in intellectual firepower aimed at imaginary targets. Nevertheless, brilliant minds were up to the challenge. Explaining the inner workings of God was a mountain to be climbed, and theologians of the age were eager to climb it.

The German theologian Rudolf Otto spoke of a *"mysterium tremendum,"* an unseen Presence apprehended in awe.[2] That's the heart of the matter.

**Mortals can *contemplate* God, and perhaps experience his presence, but we cannot *comprehend* God.** Finite minds cannot encompass infinity.

Philosophically speaking, God is a *"ding-an-sich,"*[3] a "thing-in-itself" that exists beyond the phenomenal world of sense perception. We, however, are confined within a human frame of reference, and limited to anthropomorphisms that refer to God as if "he" were human and analogies that compare "his" perceived actions to our actions. These, however, are figures of speech that attempt to describe the indescribable. Like ants

---

[1] Anselm (c. 1033-1109 CE) expressed this as *fides quaerens intellectum,* "faith seeking understanding."

[2] The concept was developed by Rudolf Otto (1869-1937) in his seminal work, *The Idea of the Holy.* It was taken up by numerous other thinkers, including Carl Jung, Martin Heidegger, Karl Barth, C.S. Lewis, Paul Tillich and Mircea Eliade.

[3] The term comes from the German philosopher Immanuel Kant (1724-1804), whose ideas influenced the fields of metaphysics, epistemology, ethics and aesthetics.

scurrying about on the ground, we're oblivious to anything beyond our field of vision. Humility, not hubris, is the pathway to
God.

# 7. Creeds left a legacy of intolerance

After Arianism was banned by the Council of Constantinople in 381 CE, Roman Catholicism was named the official religion of the Empire. Believing in "One God in three Persons"
was mandatory, and those who refused to profess that belief
were deemed guilty of *lèse majesté*, a crime against the Emperor himself punishable by death. Paganism itself was outlawed in 392 CE.[1] At that point, after centuries of external persecution and internal battles against heretics, Roman Catholicism emerged triumphant.

The church continued its intolerance of deviant beliefs in
spreading north into Europe. Untold thousands were executed
during the Spanish Inquisition for refusing to profess strict Roman Catholic beliefs.[2] Heretics were tortured and burned at the
stake. Jews, jeered as "Christ-killers,"[3] were driven from town
to town, forced into ghettoes and subjected to vicious pogroms.
Jews living in York, England, were corralled and massacred at
Clifford's Tower in 1190 CE, which still stands as a mute re-
minder of those days. Similar atrocities took place throughout
Europe in the Middle Ages.

Christians hated Muslims for conquering the Holy Land and
forcing Christians there to convert to Islam.[4] Crusades to recon-
quer the land were mounted from 1095 to 1291 CE, but all ultimately failed. Thousands of Christians and Muslims were kil-

---

[1] Walker, *History*, 117-18.
[2] The Spanish Inquisition began in the late fifteenth century and ended with
Napoleon's conquest of Spain in 1808. Wildly varying estimates of those
killed during that time range from 40,000 to over 300,000.
[3] For more on this, see the Excursus.
[4] Arab conquests in the seventh century took two-thirds of the old Roman
Empire. Jews and Christians were often allowed to continue practicing their
faith, but many were forcibly converted to Islam.

led in bloody battles during those years, leaving a legacy of hatred that persists on both sides to the present day.

Christians had no qualms about killing other Christians as well as Jews and Muslims. Protestants and Catholics engaged in ferocious battles across Europe during the sixteenth and seventeenth centuries. All died for the glory of God, knowing they alone defended the truth.

**Intolerance metastasizes.** The pogroms of the middle ages morphed into the Holocaust of the Second World War,[1] an incomprehensible tragedy in which millions of Jews were shot, burned alive, gassed and cremated.[2] Yet, despite the emaciated prisoners and piles of corpses seen at Dachau and Auschwitz, antisemitism lives on, smoldering beneath the patina of modern society. Neo-Nazis burn torches at night and murder Jews as they worship on the Sabbath.

Serbs murdered eight thousand Muslim men and boys at Srebrenica during the Bosnian War in an atrocity justified as "ethnic cleansing" to help preserve the nation's Christian heritage.

Muslims fleeing violence in the Middle East are kept from entering Europe by fences and armed guards. They languish in squalid camps, trapped, unable to move ahead and too afraid to return home, with hope for better lives ever dimming. Fleeing terrorism, the refugees are seen as terrorists.

Islamaphobia soared in the United States after the terrorist attacks on 9/11/2001. Years of fighting the Taliban in Afghanistan and al-Qaeda in Iraq followed, with ever growing hostility

---

[1] Vile *Judensau* reliefs from the Middle Ages, picturing Jews as pigs, adorn the facades of a few German churches to this day, including the Stadtkirche in Wittenberg where Martin Luther preached. Luther's treatise, *On the Jews and Their Lies*, urged Christians to burn Jewish homes, schools, synagogues and sacred books, which is precisely what took place on Kristallnacht in October, 1938.

[2] Paradoxically, Germany was said to have been the most Christianized of any European nation prior to the war.

toward Muslims. Mosques are defaced, and Muslims harassed and murdered.

But not all Muslims are terrorists. Most condemn jihadists as criminals and simply want to live in peace. Many hold moderate views of Islam. Some, like Salmon Rushdie, hold liberal views. The Koran, like the bible, is subject to various interpretation. So, not all Muslims are extremists. They can't be tarred with the same brush. Like anyone else, they deserve to be judged on the basis of their own individual merits.

Christians, of course, aren't the only ones who've committed atrocities in the name of God. People in other religions have done the same and, like Christians, bear guilt for the suffering they've caused.

**Intolerance distills into hatred and hatred congeals into violence.** No one has a corner on truth. The keys to the kingdom of God belong to all of us.

# Conclusion

Jesus of Nazareth was passionately devoted to God and guided by an unerring moral compass. He hated suffering, and was deeply moved by the misery of people living in poverty, ravaged by disease or scorned by society. Injustice angered him, and he stood up against elites who oppressed weak and powerless people. His mind was razor-sharp, and he confounded his enemies with the brilliance of his arguments.[1] By any measure, Jesus of Nazareth was an amazing human being. In fact, he was so unlike anyone ever seen that his followers began to think of him as a god. But he wasn't. He was an extraordinary man, but a man nonetheless.

That's why the dogmas of his divinity are false. His body didn't rise from the grave, and his death on a cross didn't "atone" for the sins of the world. He wasn't a divine being who came from heaven, "incarnate" in human flesh, nor an admixture of man and God while on earth. The idea of his being "*homoousion*" with God is sheer fantasy. Taken together, these dogmas paint an idolatrous picture of Jesus as God.

The Second Commandment builds on the First:

> *You shall not make for yourself an idol, whether in the form of anything that is in heaven above, or that is on the earth beneath, or that is in the water under the earth.*[2]

Not all idols are made of wood or stone. They can be *mental*, as well as physical, images of God, and reside in our minds instead of a shrine. Idolatry understood as false *ideas* about

---

[1] As seen from his debates in the temple (Mark 11:27-12:37; Matt 21:23-27, 33-45, 22:15-46; Luke 20:1-44). See also Mark 3:22-26 (Matt 12:22-27; Luke 11:14-19). The gospels cite only one instance in which Jesus lost an argument (Mark 7:26-29).
[2] Ex 20:4; Deut 5:8.

God explains why the dogmas of Christ's divinity are idolatrous. They portray a man as God, thereby breaking both the First and Second Commandments.

The historical Jesus never intended to start a religion, much less become the object of one. He was a deeply pious man who, like all Jews, believed in one God and one God alone. That was the heart of Judaism. Being worshipped as God would have been utter blasphemy![1]

As seen in the following episode, Jesus rejected human dogmas about God:

*Now when the Pharisees and some of the scribes who had come from Jerusalem gathered around him, they noticed that some of his disciples were eating with defiled hands, that is, without washing them . . . . So the Pharisees and scribes asked him, "Why do your disciples not live according to the tradition of the elders, but eat with defiled hands?" He said to them, "Isaiah prophesied rightly about you hypocrites, as it is written,*
>    *'This people honors me with their lips,*
>        *but their hearts are far from me;*
>    *in vain do they worship me,*
>        *teaching human precepts as doctrines.'*
*You abandon the commandment of God and hold to human tradition."[2]*

The Pharisees' traditions were self-serving and misrepresented God. That's why Jesus denounced them—and why, if here today, he would do the same with the dogmas of his divinity.

**Denying Jesus' divinity doesn't deny that God exists.** On the contrary, it affirms the existence of one God alone. The precedent for belief in only one God is well established. It goes all the way back to Abraham, Moses and Jesus himself.

---

[1] Cf. Acts 12:21-23.
[2] Mark 7:1-2, 5-8 (Is 29:13); Matt 15:1-9. Cf also Mark 2:27.

# EXCURSUS
## The New Testament Roots of Christian Anti-Semitism

Jesus and his disciples were Jews, and Christianity began as a sect within Judaism. But life as a sect was short-lived. As faith in Jesus spread beyond Palestine, it caught the attention of Gentiles called "God-Fearers" who worshipped alongside Jews in their synagogues. Synagogues were the first places Jewish missionaries like Paul stopped as they journeyed from town to town.[1] Jews typically rejected the message of a crucified and risen messiah, but God-fearing Gentiles in the congregation welcomed it.[2]

But that created an unforeseen problem. How could Gentiles take part in a Jewish movement? Conservatives said Gentiles had to be circumcised and follow Jewish laws.[3] Moderates disagreed, saying that was too strict and would drive Gentiles away. A compromise was reached that allowed Gentiles to join as long as they observed a few basic rules that made them acceptable to the sect's Jews.[4] However, as Gentiles continued to join the sect, it lost its original character, and Jews stopped joining the movement they began. As that transition progressed, tension grew between Jews who joined the sect and mainstream Jews who rejected it.

That growing divide accounts for the story of Jesus' trial before Pilate.[5] The stories in the gospels are fictional, not historical, and place the blame for Jesus' death on Jews instead of Pilate. Their depictions of Pilate and the crowd that allegedly called for Jesus' crucifixion make that clear.

---

[1] See, for example, Acts 13:5, 13-16, 42-43; 17:1-3; 18:4; 19:8.
[2] Acts 13:44-48; 14:1. Cf. also Acts 17:4, 10-12.
[3] The issue is highlighted in Acts 11:1-18.
[4] Acts 15:1-21. 28-29.
[5] Mark 15:1-15; Matt 27:11-26; Luke 23:1-25; John 18:28-19:16.

# Pilate

The New Testament gospels say Pilate wanted to free Jesus but backed down in the face of an angry crowd. Mark, the earliest gospel, painted the scene:

*So the crowd came and began to ask Pilate to do for them according to his custom. Then he answered them, "Do you want me to release for you the King of the Jews?" For he realized that it was out of jealousy that the chief priests had handed him over. But the chief priests stirred up the crowd to have him release Barabbas for them instead. Pilate spoke to them again, "Then what do you wish me to do with the man you call the King of the Jews?" They shouted back, "Crucify him!" Pilate asked them, "Why, what evil has he done?" But they shouted all the more, "Crucify him!" So Pilate, wishing to satisfy the crowd, released Barabbas for them; and after flogging Jesus, he handed him over to be crucified.[1]*

Matthew and Luke repeat this with a few added touches of their own.[2] Matthew added the following vignette to the story:

*While (Pilate) was sitting on the judgement seat, his wife sent word to him, "Have nothing to do with that innocent man, for today I have suffered a great deal because of a dream about him."[3]*

This is obvious fiction. The person who wrote Matthew had no way of knowing what Pilate's wife might have said in a note to her husband during the trial.

Another fictitious passage has led to unfathomable suffering over the centuries:

---

[1] Mark 15:8-15.
[2] Scholars agree that Mark was the first written gospel, and that the authors of Matthew and Luke copied Mark in writing their own gospels.
[3] Matt 27:19.

*So when Pilate saw that he could do nothing, but rather that
a riot was beginning, he took some water and washed his
hands before the crowd, saying, "I am innocent of this man's
blood; see to it yourselves." Then the people as a whole
answered,* **"His blood be on us and on our children!"** [1]

Luke repeats the assertion that Pilate wanted to free Jesus:

*Pilate then called together the chief priests, the leaders and
the people, and said to them, "You brought me this man as
one who was perverting the people; and here I have examined him in your presence and have not found this man guilty
of any of your charges against him . . . . Indeed, he has done
nothing to deserve death. I will therefore have him flogged
and release him.* [2]

Hearing this, the crowd goes berserk: "Away with this fellow!
Release Barabbas for us!"

*Pilate, wanting to release Jesus, addressed them again; but
they kept shouting, "Crucify, crucify him!" A third time he
said to them, "Why, what evil has he done? I have found in
him no ground for the sentence of death . . . . But they kept
urgently demanding with loud shouts that he should be crucified; and their voices prevailed.* [3]

"Their voices prevailed." Poor Pilate! He couldn't stand up to
an angry crowd!

The fourth gospel agrees. According to John, Pilate said, "I
find no case against him." But Jesus' accusers were implacable:
"We have a law, and according to that law he ought to die because he has claimed to be the Son of God." Hearing these
words, Pilate was then "more afraid than ever"![4] (One might
ask, of course, how the author knew what Pilate was feeling!)

---

[1] Matt 27:24-25 (my bolding).
[2] Luke 23:13-17.
[3] Luke 23:20-23.
[4] John 19:8.

*From then on Pilate tried to release him, but the Jews cried out, "If you release this man, you are no friend of the emperor. Everyone who claims to be a king sets himself against the emperor." When Pilate heard these words, he brought Jesus outside and sat on the judge's bench at a place called the Stone Pavement, or in Hebrew Gabbatha . . . . He said to the Jews, "Here is your King!" They cried out, "Away with him! Away with him! Crucify him!" Pilate asked them, "Shall I crucify your King?" The chief priests answered, "We have no king but the emperor." Then he handed him over to them to be crucified.*[1]

The accusation of being "no friend of Caesar" was a charge of treason. It was a ploy in the story line to intimidate Pilate, and it worked: Pilate "handed him over to them to be crucified." What? Pilate handed him over to *them*? That *Jews* crucified Jesus is said nowhere else in the new Testament. The statement is patently false,[2] and reveals the author's intent to blame Jews, instead of Pilate, for Jesus' death.

**The gospel stories of Jesus' trial mischaracterize Pilate.** History shows that he was as brutal as any other Roman procurator in Palestine. The idea of his being intimidated by a angry crowd is ludicrous! People who threatened Roman authority were killed without a thought.

The Gospel of Luke makes a passing comment about "Galileans whose blood Pilate had mingled with their sacrifices."[3] Galilee was a hot spot for insurrection, and Pilate assumed these men were in town to make trouble.

Flavius Josephus, a first century Jewish historian, recorded instances of Pilate's brutality.[4] One recounts how Pilate placed

---

[1] John 19:12-16.
[2] The Sanhedrin wasn't allowed to impose the death penalty. The Roman authorities reserved that right for themselves.
[3] Luke 13:1.
[4] Lester L. Grabbe, *Judaism from Cyrus to Hadrian* (2 vols.; Minneapolis: Fortress Press, 1992), 2:423-24.

military standards emblazoned with Roman eagles around the temple. Jews were enraged by seeing these stylized eagles on holy ground,[1] and rioted. They were ordered to disperse but many dropped to the ground, turned on their backs and exposed their throats to the soldiers' swords! Astounded by that act of bravery, Pilate relented and ordered his flags removed from temple ground.

The next incident was even worse. Pilate wanted to build an aqueduct into Jerusalem and stole the money to build it from the temple treasury. The temple served as a bank as well as a place of worship. Jews kept money and other valuables there for safekeeping.[2] They were enraged by Pilate's theft, and infuriated by his having trespassed on holy ground. Gentiles were forbidden on sacred ground, and signs posted around the temple warned them to stay away on pain of death.[3] But none of that bothered Pilate. He went where he pleased. He expected rioting and was ready for it. His soldiers had disguised themselves, hidden clubs under their cloaks and mingled with the crowd. When signaled, they attacked the rioters and viciously beat them, leaving many dead.

Another incident was still more deadly:

A man promised to show the Samaritans the sacred vessels of the tabernacle . . . . A large group gathered in a nearby village with the intention of climbing Mount Gerizim for the demonstration at a particular time. Whether it was anything more than a peaceful gathering is not indicated, but Pilate evidently interpreted it as the prelude of a revolt. Before they could actually make the ascent of the mountain, they were intercepted by Roman troops who killed and captured many and scattered the rest. The leaders and most prominent

---

[1] The stylized eagles broke the commandment against false images (Exod 20:4-6; Deut 5:8-10).

[2] Jeremias, *Jerusalem*, 134.

[3] Archaeologists have discovered several of these signs. One, in Greek, says: "No stranger is to enter within the balustrade round the temple and enclosure. Whoever is caught will be himself responsible for his ensuing death."

individuals among those captured were executed at Pilate's orders.[1]

**These incidents prove that the Pilate depicted in the gospels never existed.** The figure they portray is a figment of early Christian imagination. The idea that Pilate was fair and tried to free Jesus is absurd. Nothing could be further from the truth.

Crowds threatened Roman authority, and crowds followed Jesus wherever he went.[2] Messianic figures like him were eliminated to prevent insurrections.[3] So, acting preemptively, Pilate executed Jesus.

But this poses an obvious question. If Pilate was as brutal as other Roman procurators, why do the gospels portray him so favorably?

The answer is simple: *Christians didn't criticize Roman officials.* It would have been the kiss of death.

The gospels were written in the late first century[4] as Christians were just starting to be persecuted. Nero persecuted them first, followed by Diocletian and Trajan.[5] Other Roman emperors did the same over the course of the next two centuries.[6]

Nero accused Christians of starting a fire that ravaged Rome in 64 CE, and subjected them to torture. Peter was crucified

---

[1] Grabbe, *Judaism*, 2:424.

[2] The gospels cite large crowds following Jesus. (See, for example, Mark 2:4,13, 4:1, 5:21, 24, 31, 8:1; Matt 4:25, 8:1,18, 13:2, 15:30, 19:2, 20:29; Luke 7:11, 8:4,19, 9:37.)

[3] Two such messianic figures, Theudas and Judas the Galilean, are mentioned in Acts 5:36-37.

[4] Mark was written around 70 CE, Luke between 70 and 90, Matthew between 80 and 100, and John in the last decade of the first century (Kümmel, *Inroduction*, 97, 151, 119, 246).

[5] Nero persecuted Christians from 64-67 CE, Diocletian in 81 CE and Trajan in 108 CE.

[6] Christianity was an illicit (unlicensed) religion in the Roman Empire until legalized by the Edict of Milan in 313 CE.

upside down and Paul beheaded. The Roman historian Tacitus described the cruelty:

> An arrest was first made of all who confessed; then, upon their information, an immense multitude was convicted, not so much of the crime of arson, as of hatred of the human race. Mockery of every sort was added to their deaths. Covered with the skins of beasts, they were torn by dogs and perished, or were nailed to crosses, or were doomed to the flames. These served to illuminate the night . . . .[1]

The trauma of those years was still fresh when Mark was written. Would anyone have blamed Pilate for Jesus' death at a time like that? It would have antagonized Roman officials and provoked further suffering. Saying instead that Pilate knew Jesus was innocent and tried to free him was better. That would ingratiate Christians with the authorities instead of antagonizing them. Even better, why not blame someone else—like a crowd of angry Jews—for Jesus' death?

Claudius expelled Jews from Rome in 49 CE for causing disturbances in the city "at the instigation of Chrestus."[2] A war fought against Jews in Palestine lasted from 66-74 CE.[3] Jews were *personae non gratae* in the Empire and widely disliked, making them convenient scapegoats easily blamed for Jesus' death instead of Pilate.

-----

[1] Stevenson, *A New Eusebius*, 2.

[2] Stevenson, *A New Eusebius*, 1 (quotingSuetonius). "*Chrestus*" was undoubtedly a corruption of *Christos*, misunderstood as a man causing trouble among the city's Jews. As seen in Acts, Jews were typically angered by the "Good News" of a crucified and risen messiah. Paul's preaching in a synagogue in Thessalonica, for example, incited a riot in which the mob reportedly shouted, "These people who have turned the world upside down have come here also!" (Acts 17:6) It's not difficult to see the same thing happening in Rome as well.

[3] This, the Great Revolt, was followed by two others: the Rebellion of the Exile (115-17 CE) and the Bar Kochba revolt (132-36 CE). All ended in disaster, and the Jewish state ceased to exist after Rome crushed the last revolt.

# The Crowd that called for Jesus' Death

Crowds figured prominently in Jesus' last days. The first encountered was one that welcomed him to Jerusalem:

> *Many people spread their cloaks on the road, and others spread leafy branches that they had cut in the fields. Then those who went ahead and those who followed were shouting,*
> *"Hosanna!*
> *Blessed is the one who comes in the name of the Lord!*
> *Blessed is the coming kingdom of our ancestor David!*
> *Hosanna in the highest heaven!"*[1]

The shouts of *"Hosanna!"* reveal why the crowd was so excited.[2] "Hosanna" means *"Save now!"*[3] It was a cry for help, and shows that the crowd regarded Jesus as Israel's long-awaited messiah, the son of David, whose coming presaged the return of a Davidic kingdom.

Israel reached the peak of its military, economic and political power under David and Solomon in the tenth century BCE. Life was good and people prospered. Literature and the arts flourished. It was a golden age, but short-lived. Civil war broke out after Solomon's death in 922 BCE, pitting rival

---

[1] Mark 11:8-10.

[2] The exclamation comes from the Hallel (Psalms 113-18), which Jews recited as they neared Jerusalem on religious pilgrimages. The following passage from Luke shows that hope for God's help was tied to the coming of the messiah:

"Blessed be the Lord God of Israel,
 for he has looked favorably on his people and redeemed them.
He has raised up a mighty savior for us in the house of his servant David,
 as he spoke through the mouth of his holy prophets from of old,
 that we would be saved from our enemies
 and from the hand of all who hate us." (Luke 1:68-71)

[3] "Hosan_na!" combines a Hebrew verb (הושיעה) meaning "to help" or "to save" with an interjection that means "I pray!" or "now!" In this instance, as shouted by an excited crowd, the "na" (נא) at the end of "Hosan_na" is better understood as "now!"

kingdoms in the north and south of the country against each other. Assyria obliterated the northern kingdom of Israel in 722-21 BCE,[1] and Babylon conquered the southern kingdom of Judah in 587 BCE. Persia defeated Babylon in 539 BCE, and fell in turn to Alexander the Great in 331 BCE. Greek dynasties arose in Egypt (Ptolemies) and Syria (Seleucids) after Alexander died in 323 BCE. The Maccabees broke their Seleucid yoke a century later, giving Jews a brief taste of freedom that ended when Roman troops invaded the land in 64 BCE.

At that point, Jews were reduced to being captives in their own land yet again, yearning to be free. That hope explains why this crowd was elated. Jesus embodied their dreams for freedom and a new Davidic state. Seeing him, they shouted *"Hosanna!"*— *"Save NOW!"*—not from sin, but from the hated Romans occupying their land.

Matthew repeats the account of Jesus' entry into the city:

*A very large crowd spread their cloaks on the road, and others cut branches from the trees and spread them on the road. The crowds that went ahead of him and that followed were shouting,*
   *"Hosanna to the Son of David!*
   *Blessed is the one who comes in the name of the Lord!*
   *Hosanna in the highest heaven!"*[2]

"Hosanna to the Son of David!" David's kingdom was about to reappear.

Matthew adds a note to Mark's account:

*When he entered Jerusalem, the whole city was in turmoil, asking, "Who is this?" The crowds were saying, "This is the prophet Jesus from Nazareth in Galilee."*[3]

---

[1] Remembered thereafter as the "ten lost tribes" of Israel.
[2] Matt 21:8-9.
[3] Matt 21:10-11.

Word travels fast. Jews had come to Jerusalem from around the Empire, and the news of a prophet coming to town was exciting.

Luke's author deleted Mark's references to Jewish political aspirations in order to avoid offending "the most excellent Theophilus":[1]

> *As he was now approaching the path down from the Mount of Olives, the whole multitude of the disciples began to praise God joyfully with a loud voice for all the deeds of power that they had seen, saying,*
>     *"Blessed is the king who comes in the name of the Lord! Peace in heaven, and glory in the highest heaven!"*[2]

Luke universalizes Mark's account. No shouts of "Hosanna!"—"Save NOW (from Rome)!"—are heard here, and nothing is said of a new Davidic kingdom. Jesus isn't the "Son of David"; he's simply called a "king." Romans wouldn't have heard Jewish political aspirations like those as "Good News"! So, the incendiary hope for a new Davidic kingdom gave way to an innocuous hope for "peace and glory in heaven." How could anything that bland offend "the most excellent Theophilus"?

"The whole multitude of the disciples" accompanies Jesus down the Mount of Olives in Luke, but Mark and Matthew don't describe the crowd. Mark simply says that "many people" were in it, and Matthew calls it "a very large crowd."

The picture of the crowd is different in the Gospel of John:

> *The next day the **great crowd that had come to the Festival** heard that Jesus was coming to Jerusalem. So they took branches of palm trees and went out to meet him, shouting,*
>     *"Hosanna!*
>     *Blessed is the one who comes in the name of the Lord— The King of Israel!"*[3]

---

[1] Luke 1:1-4; Acts 1:1.
[2] Luke 19:37-38.
[3] John 12:12-13.

The people in this crowd are identified as *religious pilgrims in town for the festival.*

So, which gospel is right? Was the crowd composed of Jesus' *disciples*, or *religious pilgrims*? Actually, if seen as descriptions of the crowd at different points in time, both might be correct. Jesus' disciples started out with him down the Mount of Olives, and religious pilgrims, hearing the commotion, came out to join them as they neared the city. Crowds aren't static, and this one undoubtedly grew in size as Jesus approached Jerusalem. So, in all likelihood, the crowd began with Jesus' disciples, and ended with the inclusion of religious pilgrims from around the Empire.

Passover was a major festival in Jerusalem. The city's population doubled or tripled, and might even have reached a hundred thousand.[1] It's entirely conceivable, therefore, that Jesus found himself surrounded by hundreds of visiting pilgrims.

The temple was the festival's focal point.[2] People felt drawn to God there. His Spirit, his glorious *shekinah*, filled its innermost sanctum, the Holy of Holies. The temple was a sacred place for sacrifices, prayer and meditation. That was its *raison d'être,* the reason it existed.

Unfortunately, human nature has a way of subverting our best intentions and purest of motives. The priests who ran the temple got rich from fees charged for doing business on its grounds.[3] Righteous Jews like Jesus were outraged by that

---

[1] Jeremias, *Jerusalem*, 82.

[2] This was the second temple. The first temple, built by Solomon, was completed in 957 BCE and destroyed by Babylonians in 587 BCE. A modest temple replaced it in 515 BCE. Herod the Great enlarged and improved this second temple in a monumental building project that started in 20 BCE and ended forty-six years later. Roman troops razed this magnificent new edifice to the ground in 70 CE, a mere twenty-four years after its completion.

[3] Contemporary writings mention priestly avarice. Commercial transactions took place in the "Court of the Gentiles," the outermost part of the temple.

abuse of authority and castigated them for loving money more than God.[1]

Moneychangers manipulated currency exchange rates,[2] and merchants inflated the prices of sacrificial animals and religious goods. Those practices stopped when Jesus "cleansed" the temple.[3] As shown by his withering denunciation, the religious hierarchy of the temple was deeply involved in its corruption:

*Is it not written, "My house shall be called a house of prayer for all the nations"? But you have made it a den of robbers.*[4]

An accusation that scathing couldn't be ignored::

*And when the chief priests and scribes heard it, they kept looking for a way to kill him; for they were afraid of him, because the whole crowd was spellbound by his teaching.*[5]

The priests lost their fees when Jesus stopped commerce on temple ground, and they were enraged. So, how did Jesus get away with it? Why wasn't he arrested on the spot?

Jesus escaped arrest because *religious pilgrims "spellbound by his teaching" surrounded him.* Attempting to arrest him in the midst of a crowd like that would have sparked a riot.

But Jesus wasn't finished. He went on to speak against the high priests themselves in the very temple they operated! But again, adoring pilgrims surrounded him:

---

[1] Many devout Jews, including Essenes in the Dead Sea community at Qumran, forsook the temple altogether at that time.

[2] Greek and Roman money was imprinted with images and had to be exchanged for currency (Jewish and Tyrian shekels) approved by the high priests.

Hebrew scripture condemns false weights and measures (e.g. Lev 19:35-36; Deut 25:13-16; Prov 11:1, 20:10, 23; Micah 6:11; cf. Luke 6:38), which undoubtedly plagued trade in the temple as well as the city's marketplaces.

[3] Mark 11:15-17, Matt 21:12-13, Luke 19:45-46, John 2:13-17

[4] Mark 11:17, Matt 21:13, Luke 19:46 (cf. John 2:16).

[5] Mark 11:18, Luke 19:47 (cf. John 11:45-53).

*When they realized that he had told this parable against them, they wanted to arrest him, but they feared the crowd. So they left him and went away.*[1]

Matthew repeats this:

*When the chief priests and the Pharisees heard his parables, they realized that he was speaking about them. They wanted to arrest him, but they feared the crowds, because they regarded him as a prophet.*[2]

Luke says the same thing:

*When the scribes and chief priests realized that he had told this parable against them, they wanted to lay hands on him at that very hour, but they feared the people.*[3]

How could Jesus be stopped? How could the temple authorities arrest him when he was surrounded by throngs of religious pilgrims.

*It was two days before the Passover and the festival of unleavened bread. The chief priests and the scribes were looking for a way to arrest Jesus by stealth and kill him; for they said, "Not during the festival, or there may be a riot among the people.*[4]

The temple hierarchy didn't know what to do. How could they arrest Jesus without starting a riot? But that's when Judas appeared and told them how to find Jesus when he wasn't surrounded by a crowd. They could arrest him at night, outside the city, as he and his disciples slept in the Garden of Gethsemane.[5]

Look closely at what happened next. According to Mark:

---

[1] Mark 12:12.
[2] Matt 21:45-46.
[3] Luke 20:19
[4] Mark 14:1-2, Matt 26:3-5, Luke 22:1-2.
[5] Mark 14:10-11, Matt 26:14-16, Luke 22:3-6.

*Judas, one of the twelve, arrived; and with him there was* **a crowd** *with swords and clubs,* **from the chief priests, the scribes, and the elders.**[1]

Matthew echoes Mark:

*Judas, one of the twelve arrived; with him was* **a large crowd** *with swords and clubs,* **from the chief priests and the elders of the people.**[2]

Luke expands Mark:

*. . . suddenly* **a crowd** *came, and the one called Judas, one of the twelve, was leading them . . . . Then Jesus said to* **the chief priests, the officers of the temple police, and the elders** *who had come for him, "Have you come out with swords and clubs as if I were a bandit? When I was with you day after day in the temple, you did not lay hands on me. But this is your hour, and the power of darkness!"*[3]

John agrees with the other gospels:

*So Judas brought* **a detachment of soldiers together with police from the chief priests and Pharisees,** *and they came there with lanterns and torches and weapons.*[4]

All four gospels agree that Jesus was arrested by a crowd *from the temple*[5] —a crowd of *temple employees* paid by priests. The priests' fees stopped when Jesus stopped commerce on sacred soil, which in turn jeopardized the wages they paid to their employees. So, like the priests, they too had a motive for getting rid of Jesus.

**The crowd that arrested Jesus at night and the crowds that followed him during the day were entirely different.**

---

[1] Mark 14:43 (my bolding).
[2] Matthew 26:47 (my bolding).
[3] Luke 22:47, 52-53 (my bolding).
[4] John 18:3 (my bolding).
[5] Jeremias, *Jerusalem*, 138. The temple was the city's largest employer, an economic powerhouse that provided jobs for thousands of people.

141

That should be obvious. How could the same crowd shout, "Blessed is the one who comes in the name of the Lord!" and then scream, "Crucify him!" a few days later? How could the same people bless Jesus one day and curse him the next? Extreme reversals like that characterize Borderline Personality Disorder,[1] a mental illness in which a person first idealizes, and then demonizes, another. Someone with this disorder sees no shades of gray; everything is black or white. People are either good or bad, friends or foes, angels or devils. An individual with this disorder might easily shout, "Blessed is the one who comes in the name of the Lord!" one day, and "Crucify him!" the next, *but not an entire crowd.*

The feelings are mutually exclusive. We can't bless and curse someone in the same breath.

Above all, the gospels themselves identify different crowds. The crowd that screamed, "Crucify him!" as the week ended was *not* the crowd that shouted, "Blessed is the one who comes in the name of the Lord!" as it began. The two crowds were entirely different.

The Gospel of John contains an overlooked detail that identifies the "crowd" responsible for Jesus' death. It's hiding in plain sight in a passage that in the Latin Vulgate Bible declares: *"Ecce homo!"*— "Behold the Man!"

> . . . *Jesus came out, wearing the crown of thorns and the purple robe. Pilate said to them, "Here is the man!" When* **the chief priests and the police** *saw him, they shouted, "Crucify him! Crucify him!"*[2]

This is *not* the crowd that appears elsewhere in the gospels. It *isn't* a mob of ordinary Jews. It's just the *chief priests and temple police*!

---

[1] Diagnostic and Statistical Manual of Mental Disorders, 5th Edition (DSM-5 301.83).

[2] John 19:6 (my bolding).

This has the ring of truth. Ordinary Jews had no reason to hate Jesus. On the contrary, they saw him as one of their own, a freedom fighter in the struggle against Rome. The priests and their employees, on the other hand, had every reason to kill him for driving commerce off temple ground.

The temple hierarchy was keenly aware of the danger Jesus posed:

*If we let him go on like this, everyone will believe in him, and the Romans will come and destroy both our holy place and our nation.*[1]

So, there was no question. Jesus had to die.

This brings us back to Josephus, the Jewish historian. In an exhaustive history of Israel to his own time in the first century, Josephus stated that Pilate executed Jesus **"upon hearing him accused by men of the highest standing among us."**[2]

Josephus didn't say who those men were, but they undoubtedly belonged to the Great Sanhedrin,[3] Israel's supreme judicial body, which met within the temple in the Hall of Hewn Stones. The Sanhedrin was led by the High Priest, and its seventy-one members included respected "elders" of the community, Sadducees who ran the temple, and Pharisees learned in Mosaic law.

The composition of the Sanhedrin agrees with the detail in John about chief priests and temple police being responsible for Jesus' death. The point here, however, is that *neither John nor Josephus mentions a mob*. Both sources point to *a conspiracy among Jewish elites* to kill Jesus.

That "men of the highest standing" plotted Jesus' death contradicts the gospel picture of a crazed mob, but there's no

---

[1] John 11:48.

[2] Gerd Theissen and Annette Merz, *The Historical Jesus, A Comprehensive Guide* (Minneapolis: Fortress Press, 1996), 66. The quotation comes from the *Antiquities of the Jews* (*Antt.* 18,63f.) in a passage known as the Testimonium Flavianum.

[3] Other Sanhedrins of twenty-three men governed smaller towns.

reason to doubt Josephus. He had nothing to gain by inventing or falsifying his words. He simply reported what he had heard. Powerbrokers plotting Jesus' death makes more sense than ordinary Jews demanding it.

The collaboration of powerful Jews made Pilate's job easier. He would have granted a request to execute Jesus from "men of the highest standing" without a second thought. It served his own interests as well as the interests of Jewish elites.

**The notion, therefore, that Jews as a whole bear "collective guilt" for Jesus' death is false.** Jesus died because the powerbrokers of Jewish society conspired against him.

But this raises an obvious question. If a few elite Jews were responsible for Jesus' death, why were all Jews blamed for it? The answer goes back to the Gospel of Matthew, and the words it falsely attributes to a fictitious crowd:

> *Then the people as a whole answered,*
> *"His blood be on us and on our children!"*

As said at the start of this discussion, Christianity was a Jewish sect before it became a Gentile movement. As that happened, the sect lost its original Jewish character and Jews stopped joining it.

The transition was marked by conflict between Jews within the sect and Jews who refused to join it. The antipathy between those two groups of Jews explains the virulence of these words. Matthew was written by a Jewish believer in Christ who was angry at fellow Jews who refused to believe that Jesus was Israel's messiah.[1] Now, if "men of the highest standing" were responsible for Jesus' death, these words were never spoken. They weren't spoken because the crowd itself never existed— other than in the mind of an angry man. In short, *these words*

---

[1] "The author of Matthew—whose name is unknown to us—was a Greek-speaking Jewish Christian who possibly had some rabbinic knowledge but who in any case . . . accommodated the sayings of Jesus to Jewish viewpoints." (Kümmel, *Introduction*, 257)

*were invented and attributed to an imaginary crowd.* They're completely false and constitute libel against Jewish people.

### *"His blood be on us and on our children!"*

Think of all the suffering these words have caused! From the pogroms of the Middle Ages to the Holocaust and beyond, they've been used to justify countless atrocities. But the irony, the tragic irony, is that Jews never spoke them! An internecine struggle that began *among* Jews ended with the vilification of *all* Jews.

## Conclusion

The gospel stories of Christ's trial before Pilate are fictional, and falsely blame Jews, instead of Pilate, for Jesus' death. They constitute revisionist history that reflects rising hostility between church and synagogue at the start of the Common Era.

# APPENDIX A
## The Creed from Nicaea[1]  (325 CE)

We believe in one God, the Father almighty, maker of all things, visible and invisible;

And in one Lord Jesus Christ, the Son of God, begotten from the Father, only-begotten, that is, from the substance *(ousias)* of the Father,

God from God, light from light,

true God from true God, begotten not made,

of one substance *(homoousion)* with the Father,

through Whom all things came into being, things in heaven and things on earth,

Who because of us men and because of our salvation

came down and became incarnate, becoming man,

suffered and rose again on the third day,

ascended to the heavens,

and will come to judge the living and the dead;

And in the Holy Spirit.

But as for those who say,

There was when he was not,

and, Before being born He was not,

and that He came into existence out of nothing,

or who assert that the Son of God

is from a different hypostasis or substance,

or is created,

or is subject to alteration or change—

these the Catholic Church anathematizes.[2]

---

[1] The "Nicene Creed" recited today is a revised version of the original creed written at Nicaea.

[2] Kelly, *Doctrines*, 232.

# APPENDIX B

## The Creed from Chalcedon (451 CE)

We, then, following the holy Fathers, all with one consent,
teach men to confess one and the same Son, our Lord Jesus
Christ, the same perfect in Godhead and also perfect in manhood; truly God and truly man, of a Reasonable soul and body;
consubstantial *(homoousios)* with the Father
according to the Godhead,
and consubstantial *(homoousios)* with us
according to the manhood,
in all things like unto us, without sin;
begotten before all ages of the Father
according to the Godhead,
and in these latter days, for us and for our salvation,
born of the Virgin Mary, the Mother of God *(Theotokos)*,
according to the manhood;
one and the same Christ, Son, Lord, Only-begotten, in two
natures, inconfusedly, unchangeably, indivisibly, inseparably,
the distinction of natures being by no means taken away by the
union, but rather the property of each nature being preserved,
and concurring in one person and one subsistence *(hypostasis)*,
not parted or divided into two persons,
but one and the same Son and Only-begotten,
God the Word *(Logos)*, the Lord Jesus Christ;
as the prophets from the beginning have declared concerning
him, and the Lord Jesus Christ Himself has taught us, and the
creed of the holy Fathers has handed down to us.[1]

---

[1] Walker, *History*, 139.

# CITED WORKS

*American Heritage Dictionary of the English Language.* "Metaphysics" (3). 4$^{th}$ ed. Boston: Houghton Mifflin Company, 2000.

Bettenson, Henry, ed. *Documents of the Christian Church.* London: Oxford University Press, 1963.

Cross, F.L., ed. *The Oxford Dictionary of the Christian Church.* London: Oxford University Press, 1958.

De Vaux, Roland. *Ancient Israel: Its Life and Institutions.* Translated by John McHugh. New York: McGraw-Hill, 1961.

*Dialogues of Plato.* Translated by B. Jowett. New York: Random House, 1937, 17$^{th}$ ed.

Grabbe, Lester L. *Judaism from Cyrus to Hadrian.* 2 vols. Minneapolis: Fortress Press, 1992.

Harnack, Adolf. *Outlines of the History of Dogma.* Translated by Edwin Knox Mitchell. Beacon Hill, Boston: Beacon Press, 1959.

Hutchins, Robert Maynard, Editor in Chief. *Great Books of the Western World.* Translated by Samuel Butler. 4 vols. Chicago: William Benton, 1952.

Jeremias, Joachim. *Jerusalem in the time of Jesus, An Investigation into Economic and Social Conditions during the New Testament Period.* Translated by F. H. and C. H. Cave. Philadelphia: Fortress Press, 1975.

Kelly, J. N. D. *Early Christian Doctrines.* New York: Harper & Brothers, 1958.

Kittel, Gerhard, and Gerhard Friedrich, eds. *Theological Dictionary of the New Testament.* Translated by Geoffrey W. Bromiley. 10 vols. Grand Rapids: Eerdmans, 1964-1976.

Kümmel, Werner Georg. *Introduction to the New Testament.* Translated by Howard Clark Kee. Nashville: Abingdon Press, 1975.

Latourette, Kenneth Scott. *A History of Christianity.* New York: Harper and Row, 1953.

Liddell, Henry George and Robert Scott. *A Lexicon,* abridged from Liddell and Scott's *Greek-English Lexicon.* Oxford: Clarendon Press, 1974.

Richardson, Cyril C., ed. *Early Christian Fathers.* Vol. 1 in The Library of Christian Classics. Translated by Cyril C. Richardson. Philadelphia: The Westminster Press, 1953.

Robinson, J. M. "Ascension." Pages 245-47 in vol. 1 of *The Interpreter's Dictionary of the Bible.* Edited by G. A. Buttrick. 4 vols. Nashville: Abingdon, 1962.

Rylaarsdam, J. C. "*Passover and Feast of Unleavened Bread.*" Pages 663-68 in vol. 3 of *The Interpreter's Dictionary of the Bible.* Edited by G. A. Buttrick. 4 vols. Nashville: Abingdon, 1962.

Shaw, Gregory Shaw. "Ascension of Christ." Pages 61-62 in *The Oxford Companion to the Bible.* Edited by Bruce M. Metzger and Michael D. Coogan. New York: Oxford University Press, 1993.

Stevenson, J., ed. *A New Eusebius: Documents Illustrative of the History of the Church to A.D. 337.* London: S·P·C·K, 1963.

Theissen, Gerd and Annette Merz, *The Historical Jesus, A Comprehensive Guide.* Minneapolis: Fortress Press, 1996.

Thilly, Frank. *A History of Philosophy.* Revised by Ledger Wood. New York: Holt, Rinehart and Winston, 1962.

Walker, Williston. *A History of the Christian Church.* Revised by Cyril C. Richardson, Wilhelm Pauck and Robert T. Handy. New York: Charles Scribner's Sons, 1959.

Weber, Eugen, ed., *The Western Tradition*: *From the Ancient World to Louis XIV*, vol I. Lexington, MA: D.C. Heath, 1995, 5<sup>th</sup> ed.